ORGANIC COMPANION PLANTING IN SMALL SPACES

ALL-IN-ONE GUIDE TO A HIGHER HARVEST FOR YOUR FAMILY USING RAISED BED SQUARE FOOT GARDENING

KRISTY BIRD

To My Mom

Thanks for teaching me the how to garden and to follow my dreams.

CONTENTS

JUST FOR YOU

A FREE GIFT TO OUR READERS

Scan the QR code below to get The Ultimate Gardening Tool Kit.

BONUS COLORED PDF

Would you like to have access to colored pictures? Download the colored PDF version of this book. Go to https://bit.ly/3NE0LuF or scan the QR code. This comes in handy for chapters 5 and 6.

INTRODUCTION

"The glory of gardening: hands in the dirt, head in the sun, heart with nature. To nurture a garden is to feed not just the body, but the soul."

— ALFRED AUSTIN

What does it mean when you say, "two heads are better than one?" As humans, it is not uncommon for people to reach out to friends or family for support. No man is an island - plants agree with this statement. When you plant different crops together, they support one another to grow and fight pests or diseases. This is what companion planting is all about.

As a millennial, I am exposed to a lot of unhealthy foods. A 2013 article by Kai Ryssdal, a Marketplac.org senior editor, states that processed foods make up approximately seventy percent of Americans' diet. He further quotes author and journalist Melanie Warner who affirms that scientists and marketing executives at food companies would like to sell healthier food, but it is not easy. Unfortunately, the reality of our 21st-century life is that three out of every five food items we buy are unhealthy. This is why, for almost two decades, I have committed to growing my own food in my home garden.

As one who likes to maintain a healthy lifestyle, I understand the need to eat healthily. I therefore took it upon myself to discover the best way to grow healthy foods.

 Now here's something that will blow your mind: would you believe it if I told you that Prince Charles gardens? Yes, you read that right. His thirty-seven acres of organic gardens produce enough fruits and vegetables for Britain's royal family. But, of course, Prince Charles isn't the only famous person who is into gardening. Oprah Winfrey, Julia Roberts, Jessica Alba, Oscar De La Renta, and many other celebrities also grow their own food.

The Covid-19 pandemic, which necessitated a global lockdown, resulted in a shortage in supplies. Food was one of the things that became difficult to get. As the lockdown came into effect and, with it, the need to create bonding activities for families, many people turned to gardening. A press release by Packaged Facts' National Online Consumer Survey in 2021 revealed that thirty-nine percent of the American population surveyed were involved in gardening. Although twenty-six percent of this population agreed that they started growing their own food because of the pandemic, thirteen percent did not agree. Like me, thirteen percent of Americans surveyed either started gardening before the pandemic or chose to grow their own food for other reasons.

Whether you started gardening because of the pandemic, the truth remains that this is one of the most rewarding activities in the history of humanity. It is important for individuals and families to find wholesome ways of maintaining healthy lifestyles. Thankfully, gardening is one activity that cuts across all aspects of human life for healthy living.

While gardening is a potent antidepressant, it has also been proven to positively impact moods, energy levels, and sociability. Gardening appears to provide positive therapeutic and psychological benefits. With gardening, you will develop better attention and cognitive skills. As you revel in this rewarding blend of nature and nurture, you'll experience a sense of satisfaction and feel attuned to the  world. Gardening helps you fight illness, improves your memory, helps with addiction recovery, and many other benefits too numerous to mention. You can never go wrong with gardening.

We may all have different hobbies, very few encourage a healthy lifestyle. In this respect, gardening is a wonderful activity. Unfortunately, getting used to gardening best practices takes a lot of trial and error. Navigating this rewarding but dynamic terrain was difficult for me in my early years. But guess what? When I got used to the tricks and hacks, it became a natural indulgence that I wouldn't do without. With more years of experience, learning, and unlearning came expertise.

Talking about trials and errors- companion planting is one aspect of gardening that involves strict observation, trials, and mistakes. This type of gardening doesn't follow strict scientific rules. It conforms to the dynamics of each garden's uniqueness as a diverse ecosystem where plants relate as one big family that depend on one another. As someone with years of experience and well-versed in gardening, I have curated the following chapters of this book to explain how to grow healthy crops with companion planting.

Fighting diseases and pests is one of the significant problems every gardener faces. In the following chapters, you will learn how to use companion planting for weed, pest, and disease management. You will also discover how to prepare and apply composts to the soil, the watering and light requirements for different plants, which plants grow together best, and which mistakes to avoid. Finally, you will be given some planting guidelines and learn about square foot and raised bed gardening. These topics are sure to make your companion planting endeavor easy and enjoyable.

 Although this planting system has been around for years, farmers didn't know enough about it, nor did they understand the hazards of using artificial chemicals to combat pests and diseases. I can only imagine how terrible you felt when your crops died after using pesticides in your garden or when your crops didn't grow properly. You are not alone. This has happened to the best of us. Unlike those of us who had to learn the hard way, this book makes gardening easy and fun.

Now you are on the right track to learning how to use one stone to kill several birds (to use a cliché). By following the detailed steps and tips in this book, you will save limited garden space and harvest healthy crops at the end of the planting season by simply planting different crops together. These plants will form a natural support system for each other, deter pests, attract beneficial insects, improve soil fertility, and regulate shade and lightening. Did you just ask how? Follow me through the next chapters of this book to find out!

1

AN INTRODUCTION TO COMPANION PLANTING

Many people get excited when they hear it's planting season. Harvesting time brings even greater happiness, knowing you will be reaping the benefits of your hard work. I can never contain my joy when it's the season for planting. I grew up eating food grown in my mother's garden, and eating these healthy foods has significantly impacted me. Since my family is important to me, I have decided that my children, too, will eat nutritious foods grown in my own garden.

Working in the garden has helped me maintain a healthy lifestyle in every way. This is because I eat fresh foods and not chemically produced foods, and I also keep myself busy working in my garden. Gardening helps boost my mood and, at the same time, it is a good form of exercise.

I believe that you can enjoy these same benefits if you understand the idea of companion planting. So, this chapter will introduce you to these concepts and principles. This chapter will also explain the many benefits of companion planting and the advantages of growing your food organically in your garden.

WHAT IS COMPANION PLANTING?

What is the literal meaning of "companion?" It simply means "a person you spend your time with and share every memory with." It may refer to friends supporting you and protecting you from bad things and vice versa. In the end, you are benefiting from your friend's companionship, and your friend is benefiting from yours.

So, companion planting refers to different plants being grown together for their mutual benefit. The keywords in this definition are "different plants," "grown together," and "mutual benefit." Companion planting implies growing a variety of plants. This practice is not as complicated as it may seem, and it could even be as simple as planting a nectar-rich flower near your crops to attract pollinators.

Another example of companion planting is planting winter squash, climbing beans, and corn together. The winter squash shades the ground to prevent moisture loss, and its big, prickly leaves discourage weeds and pests. Climbing beans are nitrogen fixers, and they provide nitrogen to other plants. At the same time, the corn supports the climbing beans.

Companion planting has been called by a variety of names, including polyculture, and intercropping. A lot of gardeners use these names interchangeably. There are many reasons to practice companion planting. Let's list a few.

REASONS TO PRACTICE COMPANION PLANTING

Pest Prevention

Some plants have chemical or physical qualities that repel pests and some herbivorous animals. Borage is a fantastic example of a plant that may be grown with squash or pumpkins. The essential oil produced by this annual leafy plant is known to prevent the appearance of the squash bug, an awful squash and pumpkin pest.

The aromatic herb rosemary, for example, is thought to prevent the cabbage moth, whose larvae are known to harm broccoli and other cruciferous plants. Even bigger animals like rabbits, rats, and squirrels avoid plants like garlic, onions, cucumbers, and peppermint because they find them unpleasant, stinky, or thorny. So, having these plants in your garden will prevent these pests.

Soil Fertility

Some plants are nutrient accumulators, while others, thanks to their extensive tap root system, assist in the uptake of nutrients from deep soil. They nourish the soil and help their neighbors grow. Another way companion planting boosts the earth is by keeping the ground wet and preventing erosion. For instance, shading the soil may be beneficial during a drought, and cucumber and squash plants are excellent at shading the ground.

Some vegetable plants help other plants thrive by improving the soil quality. For example, beans help replenish nitrogen in the soil as they grow, and they do this by increasing the availability of nitrogen in the ground. Therefore, plants that need high nitrogen levels will benefit significantly from having beans near them.

Weed Control

Companion plants can help your primary crop by functioning as a natural cover, protecting bare soil from weeds. If you don't want weeds to grow in a particular place, plant a different plant there to let the weeds know that the spot is already occupied. It will become even more successful if you get a head start on the weeds in your garden by planting a crop that will take up space just before they start growing.

An excellent example of this is growing kale and beans together. Growing these two plants together will help prevent troublesome weeds like redroot pigweed compared to cultivating the two crops separately.

A BRIEF HISTORY OF COMPANION PLANTING

Before going into the concepts of companion planting, let's take a brief look at the history of companion planting. Companion planting is not a new notion; according to some people, it began in the 1970s with the organic movement. At that time, planting crops in different combinations to help them grow or protect them became popular, but companion planting has a long history.

A deeper look at companion planting shows that this concept was used by the ancient Greeks and Romans approximately two thousand years ago to increase their grape fields for wine production. However, the Native Americans knew about companion planting around six to eight thousand years before then.

The Chinese Companion Planting

Companion planting has been used in China for approximately two thousand years. The use of mosquito ferns on rice fields is a famous example. The ferns absorb nitrogen from the air and keep other plants from competing with the rice by blocking sunlight.

The Greeks and Romans Companion Planting

According to Marcus Terentius Varro's book on Agriculture, the Romans and Greeks were well aware of certain plants' impact on others nearby. Some of these impacts were positive, while others were negative. For instance, the Romans noticed that planting cabbages near grapevines would harm the grapevine, and any plant planted near walnut trees stopped growing.

This is because walnut and cabbages secret toxin substances into the soil to inhibit the growth of a nearby plant. The process of secreting toxin substances into the ground is known as allelopathy. The Romans used and developed this information.

The Indigenous American Companion Planting

This is the oldest known companion planting, and it has been in use for approximately eight thousand years. The three sisters, which comprise a mixed crop of beans, squash, and corn, is the most common planting method. The corn is the first to be planted, and then beans and squash are added once the corn is a few inches high.

Like the mosquito fern, beans are great at absorbing nitrogen from the air and storing it in the soil. The corn benefits from the nitrogen, while the squash keeps the weeds away. In return, the corn provides something for the beans and squash to climb on.

COMPANION PLANTING AND THE ORGANIC GARDENING MOVEMENT

The organic movement began in the early part of the twentieth century due to a significant agricultural advancement that depended entirely on chemicals such as herbicides, pesticides, and fertilizers. Companion planting was rediscovered during this organic rebirth, and the world began to experiment with new (old) approaches.

REASONS TO GROW YOUR OWN ORGANIC FOOD

Sometimes you may get tired of going to the store to get food. You may even worry about the number of chemicals and fertilizers used to grow the food you eat. I can confirm that you are not the only one with these concerns. I have been there. I grew up eating garden foods, and whenever I am away from home, I worry about the food I eat. When I got married, I began to worry about my children. This is one of the many reasons I decided to start growing my own food.

If you have decided to grow your own food in your garden or are contemplating growing your food, here are the reasons you should get to your garden for planting. It does not matter whether your garden is small or big. You won't regret growing your food. Let's take a quick look.

Homegrown Food Taste Better

You may not understand the difference unless you taste homegrown vegetables. You may not even want to go back to buying fruits and vegetables from the big supermarket once you realize how much better homegrown food tastes. Nothing is as soothing as eating a fresh tomato straight from your garden. Why do fruits and vegetables produced at home have a better taste? Let me explain.

Fruit and vegetables sold in supermarkets were usually specifically culti-vated for commercial use. These vegetables are chosen and developed with particular characteristics that make them more suitable for commercial cultivation. Generally, all the fruits mature at the same time. They are even the same shape and size. It is as if the fruits are programmed. But since they are cultivated for commercial purposes, the fruits and vegetables tend to ripen on the road. Sometimes, the chemical used in growing the fruits may also reduce the taste quality.

You Can Grow Different Crops

While supermarkets provide a wide variety of food, many are planted out of season and shipped worldwide before reaching you. However, if you grow your food instead of buying food that has been imported from all over the world, you can choose to plant a wide variety of fruits and vegetables. You can cultivate hundreds of different types of seeds in your garden. It is your choice.

You Don't Need Pesticides to Control Growth

Pests are harmful to crops and can wipe out an entire garden. Therefore, you may need some pesticides and chemicals to control them. However, since you are not practicing commercial farming, there are alternative ways of controlling pests instead of chemicals and pesticides. Here are some examples of an organic approach to dealing with pests on your garden farm.

Beneficial Insects: Beneficial insects are insects that prey on pests that are harmful to your garden. The "Lady-bug" or ladybird beetle is an example of a beneficial insect. They eat some of the bugs you don't want in your garden. Beneficial insects are consid-

erably better and safer for your garden, and boosting their existence is one of the main reasons to start growing organic.

Water Spray: You can spray water or a diluted soap solution to remove pests like aphids and similar pests.

Natural Predation: Natural predators, like beneficial insects, kill the pests in your garden. Examples of natural predators include frogs, birds, and hedgehogs.

Companion Planting: Situate different plant species close to each other to attract natural predators to feast on pests or hide vulnerable plants. One example of this is the marigold. Marigolds can be placed next to almost any plant in your garden.

Barriers or Deterrents: Guiding your plants with barriers like broken eggshells or copper ripping are organic ways of controlling pests. You can also attach straws to the base of a plant.

Hand Picking: Although handpicking may be time-consuming, it is the best method to get closer to your garden. It can also be therapeutic.

There Is Less Chance of Having Food Contamination

There is no fear of contamination if you grow fruit and food in your garden. You will be sure of where your food came from, and you can enjoy it fresh.

Seasonal Food

Eating what you produce in your garden teaches you about what is in season, and you will appreciate the fact that you are eating it when the freshness and taste are at their peak. You can learn how to preserve or can any extra fruit and vegetable. This is an added advantage.

Gardening Is Good for Your Health

Growing your own food in your garden is beneficial to your health in many ways. To begin with, gardening means that you spend every day outside in the sunlight and fresh air. Gardening is also a wonderful exercise because it necessitates a lot of flexibility and strength. Weeding, planting, and burrowing are all low-impact activities. Five minutes of gardening expends the same energy as fifteen minutes of jogging.

Gardening is an excellent way to get some physical activity and enhance your health. It reduces stress, relaxes tension, and increases energy levels. Avoiding pesticide-laden foods is also good for your health.

Gardening Can Save You Money

There is no need for expensive pots, intricate plant baskets, or other gardening accessories. Just start with the essentials, and you will maximize the returns on your investment by growing the fruit and vegetables you want to eat. Even a little plot that produces a few vegetables can save money.

 Take a bag of supermarket-bought organic strawberries. Compared that price to a package of seeds, and some soil. Plant them, care for them, and you will enjoy strawberries for at least two months, if not longer, for the same price.

Less Food Waste

Most of the fruit and veggies you pick from your garden shouldn't go to waste. The great majority of it will be eaten or preserved. Any leftovers, scraps, or peelings produced may be fed to the animals or even thrown into the compost pile to be restored to the land later as fertilizer.

Protecting Future Generations

Your current eating choices influence your child's health in the future. According to studies, children who consume a regular "supermarket" diet have more significant amounts of some pesticides in their urine than children who consume an organic diet. Children are at a higher risk than the general population because they consume more calories in terms of body weight.

Organic Produce Is Better for the Environment

You can reduce your environmental impact in various ways by growing your own food, for example, saving energy, protecting water quality, preventing soil erosion, and promoting biodiversity.

SUMMARY

If you followed this chapter in detail, you would know it is an excellent idea to grow food in your garden. Apart from the economic advantage, you can be sure of eating fresh and chemical-free food.

This chapter has introduced you to the concept of companion planting. Combining two or more plants for a specific purpose. One purpose can be used to prevent pests or insects from attacking your plants. It can also help to attract beneficial insects to your garden.

Some plants just do well when growing together. They do not compete for root space, nutrients, or sunlight. They support and help each other grow in a win-win situation. When different plants are cultivated in your garden, they work harmoniously to build the nutrients needed to survive. If the right plants are planted near each other, they will flourish.

The next chapter will show you how to prepare and plan your companion garden using raised beds and square foot gardening methods. Take another glance at this chapter and dive into the second chapter for a more in-depth examination of companion planting.

GETTING STARTED: THE PREPARATION AND PLANNING PHASE

Y ou have now decided to grow food in your garden. You know that companion planting is an excellent strategy for growing organic foods. The next thing to do is prepare and plan. This chapter will highlight the steps required to prepare and plan for a companion garden using the raised bed and square gardening methods.

It is not enough to plan and prepare for companion planting: you must also know the dos and don'ts of gardening. I remember talking to one of my childhood friends about gardening. After our talk, she promised to start a garden if I visited her during the holidays, and I agreed. She also promised to order seeds the following day.

As the holidays approached, I called to inform her that I would be on the next flight. When she picked me up at the airport, I did not ask her about the garden as I preferred to see it in person rather than have her describe it to me. As soon as we got to her house, I decided to walk around.

After a while, we took our seats on a bench close to her garden. This was where I told her most of what I will share here in this book. She mentioned she had little experience or knowledge. She was a little disappointed in her garden. Our conversation made me realize that it was easier for me when I planted a garden in my new house. I already had some experience in gardening.

As a new gardener with no experience or knowledge, there is a high probability that you may be confused and might not know how to build a raised bed or know what companion planting even is. You may not know how to pick the best location in your house for gardening. All these need to be considered before starting. In the same way that I advised my friend, it is imperative to thoroughly plan your garden so that you can make the best use of the available space. So, do not rush into your garden after deciding to start a garden. Instead, sit down, plan, and map out the steps required.

CHOOSING THE PERFECT LOCATION FOR YOUR GARDEN

The first step in starting a new garden is determining where to plant. This is because the garden's location influences the type of seed you can grow, how easy it will be to manage, and how the garden will look. In other words, the perfect location for your gardening determines how successful your gardening experience will be. For example, a food garden may be out of sight, but a flower garden may be in plain view. After all, what good are those beautiful roses and vibrant flowers if nobody can see them?

However, you may need to choose between your personal goals and the requirements of the garden you are nurturing. A garden with stunted growth and fading flowers will not offer much visual appeal and may even diminish its value. You need a healthy garden; therefore, picking a spot with enough sun, drainage, and a water supply should be prioritized. It is an added advantage if you have rich soil in the selected location. However, if that earth is not of good quality, you can always improve the richness with a bit of effort and a small investment in soil supplements.

Hopefully, you agree that choosing the perfect location should be the first thing on your planning list. So, how do you choose the ideal place? What factors should you consider when selecting the perfect location? Without waiting for the drum rolls, let's consider the requirements.

Light Requirements

Examine your home for spots that receive the maximum sunlight as you choose where to site your garden. For many plants, the ideal position gets a minimum of six hours of light every day, but that is just the bare minimum. Almost all plants you would like to grow will need even more direct sunlight. If your space is mainly shaded, look for plants with vibrant leaves and bright blossoms that will grow in a shade garden.

It is advisable to start planning your garden many months before you start so that you can observe and take note of how the sun moves throughout the seasons. Some spots may receive the required six hours of sunshine in the summer. But, when the sun drops in the spring and fall, these places may be obscured by trees, reducing direct sunlight exposure significantly. As a result, you may not be able to grow early bloomers or late-season crops.

The perfect garden site is on the south side of your house or directly adjacent to an old barn. If that fails, plant on the east side to capture the rising morning sun or on the west side to get the afternoon sun as a third alternative. If you cannot find a sunny area, trim some trees or, as the last option, create a container garden so you may move plants as required. A sunlight calculator is a handy tool to help you figure this out.

Choose a Location Near the Water

You should consider planting your garden near an existing tap to prevent having to run long lengths of pipe or hose from the tap on the side of your house. A long hose may get in the way of cleaning your garden or deteriorate in the sun. If you do not have a tap

nearby, consider putting in subsurface plumbing that will allow one to be built. Your garden will require a lot of water, particularly immediately after seeding. You do not want to rely on rain, which is sometimes insufficient to meet the demands of a garden. You will need a water supply that is easily accessible.

If this is your first garden, you will likely want to start with a small plot of land, so that you can give all of the plants the attention they require while honing your gardening skills. However, if you are more experienced or want to grow vegetables that need a lot of room, such as squash, you may decide on a bigger garden.

Consider having more than one accessible water supply if you plan a large garden, so you do not have to run a longer hose to the other end of the garden. If you do not want to build underground pipes, one option is to lay a polyethylene pipe around the garden's perimeter and connect it to an existing water supply. You can then connect to this pipe and put a tap anywhere you need water.

Look for an Airy, Not Windy Place

Some of the most dangerous diseases home gardeners face are mildew and mold on plants. Providing enough air circulation is the most efficient way to prevent this. This would indicate that the ideal garden location is more or less open to the air. Still, you don't want to subject your flowers and vegetables to severe winds either.

If you live in a location with high winds, try placing the garden on the trailing edge of a natural wind (the side away from the wind). A clump of shrubs or a wooden fence will shield them from the prevailing winds. Consider erecting a little wall around the garden to keep the wind at bay if nothing else works. Just ensure that it is not so high that it blocks the sun. You may also use the fence to hold peas and other climbing legumes. If it is sturdy enough, you might even be able to use it to raise melons and squash, saving space in the garden.

If your neighborhood's typical winds are from the north or west, you may use existing trees as windbreaks. Make sure they are not blocking the morning sunlight and do not give too much shade.

Pay Attention to the Drainage

A vegetable or flower garden should be planted on level ground so that water can sink into the soil and reach the roots. Avoid situating the garden near the bottom of a slope, especially if the ground is damp after the rain. Most plants prefer well-draining soil, as waterlogged soil causes their roots to rot. However, a few exceptions include the native perennial swamp hibiscus, which thrives in moist and wet soils and produces gigantic six-inch red or white pinwheel-shaped blooms that butterflies like.

Similarly, you do not want your garden on hilly terrain, as the plants would not receive enough water. If you only have sloping terrain, consider terracing the slopes to trap moisture. You could also construct an underground drainage system to keep water from accumulating in the terraces. You may also want to expand your garden beyond the flat spaces.

Make Your Garden Accessible

Do not situate your garden in a difficult-to-reach location because you will be visiting it every day, or at least every two days. You should not have to chop your way through the heavy bush or climb a high slope to get to the garden. Apart from the fact that it will be stressful and tiring for you, remember that you will be using a wheelbarrow in your garden. You will be transporting dirt, manure, and compost into the garden and dead leaves out of it using that wheelbarrow.

Pick a Spot With Good Soil

It is not a contest to choose between land with stony or sandy soil and one with fertile, rich, and productive loam. Naturally, you will pick loamy soil so that your plants will thank you for a choice well made.

Poor soil is not always a game-changer if you have a location within reach that satisfies most other criteria, such as enough sunshine, proximity to water, and decent visual exposure. You can add soil supplements if necessary. However, that requires more labor, and you might have to bring in compost and new soil.

Before creating a new garden, you should conduct a soil test. You can do it yourself with a kit bought in the store or collect a sample and send it to a lab for testing. You can send it to a local university near you or a garden center lab. This test will reveal the pH of the soil and how much essential nutrients your plants require to create vibrant flowers and nutritious vegetables.

If the soil test result indicates significant nutrient shortages, or if the soil is predominantly clay and does not drain properly, you should consider moving your garden or planting in raised beds. Composting can only treat nutrient-deficient soil up to a point. We will cover the details of soil in chapter three.

Look for Signs of Varmints

 Look for rodent holes as you go around your potential plant space. These are simple to see, and if you live in a rodent-infested region, don't be surprised if there are so many tunnels that the dirt crumbles beneath your feet as you walk around. If you truly want to plant your garden in that location, you should consider raised beds since each plant will require its own rodent-wire net to guard it.

Rabbits and rats may also be a problem, but you cannot tell where they will appear, unlike varmints. You can keep them away using insect repellent and flowers like sweet alyssum and marigolds, which repel rabbits. These creatures may ruin your garden, and it is worse if a digging rodent is already on your land. You should consider relocating your garden to another portion to avoid future problems.

Plant on Your Own Property

This may sound self-evident, but it is not yours if you plant on a neighbor's land and risk losing your prized vegetables and food. If you are unsure of your boundary or feel your plant may grow into a neighbor's land, you have two options. The first option is to talk to the neighbor. Check if they will agree to you planting on their land. You may even have to promise them a portion of the harvest to accept the offer. If the first option does not yield the desired result, relocate your garden.

It is always better to be the proud owner of a small piece of land than to get into trouble with a neighbor after you have worked to have a lovely garden. Your garden should bring you fresh food and peace, not problems and headaches.

PLANTING A SMALL GARDEN

Generally, planting a garden is done on your own property, whether or not it is fenced. No matter what the size, whether the space is big or small, it can be used to establish a garden. However, as previously stated, the most important thing is adequate and proper planning. The owner of a small garden may utilize and maximize their small plot of land if there is sufficient planning. I cannot stress that enough.

Although people often disagree on what defines a small garden, the odds are that many of us have a smaller area than we would prefer. There are, however, several ways to plant a small garden. To develop a small and beautiful garden of your choice, consider how you might improve the outdoor area that you already have. In addition, planting a small garden is less stressful and time-consuming.

Some of the factors to consider when planting a small garden include:

Be Inspired to Find Your Style

Study is essential at the outset of planning a small garden in order to create an appealing and functional space that looks wonderful all year. For inspiration, visit as many public grounds as possible. Although you may not see something that excites you, that does not mean you will not get ideas about the style you want in your garden.

Yearly exhibitions like the Chelsea Flower Display and the RHS Hampton Court Palace Flower Show are packed with little show gardens created by landscape gardeners to make the most of small gardens.

Designing a style guide to experiment with plant species, exterior paint colors, and furniture options are innovative ideas once you decide on your garden layout, whether it is a cottage retreat or a family refuge.

Survey and Measure Your Plot

When planning a small garden layout, whether you are beginning with a new garden or inheriting an established enclosure that needs remodeling, make a wish list and include any significant challenges. Would you prefer a dining space, for example? Do you need to fix a leaky pipe or develop ideas to make your area appear larger?

To determine its potential, measure and examine your garden. Consider where the sun rises and sets during the day and how the space may change in the coming years. Consider how your planting strategy will evolve or fade over time.

Pick Out Layout Ideas

A unique pattern will establish the foundations of your small garden, depending on its size. The most effective gardens are circular, diagonal, or rectangular, and you may add landscaping and variations on these concepts to personalize your environment. Informal gardens feature curving and flowing edges, whereas formal gardens have straight edges and symmetry.

Put Your Plan on Paper

Making errors on paper is not expensive, so start with a scaled drawing of the garden as you have measured it. Then, add your ideas as individual sections that you can move around. Alternatively, search online for a garden planner. This tool will let you enter measurements and digitally envision your ideal spot.

Create Beautiful Boundaries

Most small gardens are surrounded by fences and walls which are sometimes neglected, so careful planning of hard landscaping and borders may be as vital as the greenery. Look for solutions to this problem, such as using garden decking for a smooth finish.

Make a highlight of the boundary if the view beyond the garden is attractive. Moderate fences will allow you to see the scenery and feel that your garden is endless. Rather than using tight planks, use a traditional picket design or a contemporary slatted fence.

PREPARE A PLANTING PLAN

The planting selections bring character, form, and softness to the garden. At the same time, the hard landscaping and borders create structure. Allow for movement between the shrubbery and boundaries instead of confining the plants to the margins, which may confine the area. Create a space that complements its surroundings. Before buying, do some research into the height, spread, and soil preference of the plants you select. To create a cohesive style, stick to a single color palette. Match your flower colors with painted garden furniture, outdoor cushions, and rugs in one or two matching tones.

HOW TO DESIGN A SMALL GARDEN

With today's busy lifestyle, the garden, no matter how small, forms part of our homes and must be flexible. When designing your garden, choose portable, multi-purpose garden furniture that can be used for relaxing and partying.

If you want to make the most of your small garden, buy folding furniture for dining so you can pack it or cover it when not in use. Alternatively, choose something smaller that can be used for casual meals and relaxing, such as small lounge chairs and a coffee table. Consider adding an attraction that will give you a different view when relaxing in your garden. This can include a tree, a water feature, or even a wall painting.

If you would prefer to stay simple, a small garden plot with nothing else will still be great.

HOW TO GROW FOOD IN A SMALL GARDEN

If there is one thing I understand even more than gardening, it is growing food in small gardens. As mentioned above, I grew up in a family that loves eating organic food from the garden. I want to share my knowledge about growing food in small spaces, and I will share some of that knowledge below:

Vertical Gardening

A great solution for small space gardening is vertical gardening. You can use a trellis for this purpose. A framework can be made out of virtually anything, but I like bamboo since it is flexible and appealing. You can grow melons vertically and squash and cucumbers on your trellis.

There is a high probability that your cucumbers will flourish if you carefully train them on the trellis. I also have used hanging planters in the past, and when the weather turned chilly, I was able to bring my tomato plants inside to extend the growing cycle. Every year, I cultivated four or five cherry tomato plants.

Container Gardening

Container gardening is easy for small gardens, giving you a substantial advantage. Unlike in a typical garden, you have more control over moisture and soil content. The only thing limiting you with container gardening is your imagination: you can grow almost anything. For example, my friend is planting tomatoes in a container this year, even though she has a big garden around her house.

She has more control over the pests and soil and does not need to dig up as much ground. She has also created unique elevated beds that she will continue to expand vertically as my tomato plants mature.

Consider Plants That Do Well in Shady Areas

Small gardens have the advantage of allowing you to choose plants that thrive in shaded conditions. If you trellis your cucumbers vertically, you may put lettuce in a container beneath the cucumber trellis.

You can eat fresh lettuce when regular gardeners cannot because it is too hot outside. Their garden is in direct sunlight. Herbs may also be grown in this shaded place. Shade-tolerant herbs include parsley, mint, and oregano.

Window Farming

A window farm is a type of farm grown vertically and functions all year. This type of farming entails growing food on windowsills indoors. It necessitates some farmer interaction, but this farming technique allows you to effortlessly grow your crops hydroponically and in all seasons, even if you live in a small space. The primary purpose of window farming is to inspire city folk to produce their own food year-round within their homes. With window farming, people will be able to enhance their quality of life dramatically and live a healthier lifestyle.

So, how does this system operate in practice? The water pump is controlled by a timer and pumps nutrients through the plant columns. A lift system transports water from the bottom water supply to the upper plant bottle, driven by an air pump. Water then flows down from one bottle to the next, passing through the sticky roots of the plants, collecting any unabsorbed nutrients before flowing straight down to the lowest reservoir's bottle. The hydroponic method entails pumping nutrient-rich water from the bottom reservoir to each bottle, wetting all the plants' roots.

Water that has not been absorbed accumulates within the reservoir and is pushed out later. Hydroponically grown plants have thick and hairy roots, whereas soil-grown plants have deep and broad ones. This technique is particularly efficient since the roots are tiny and take very little space.

A window farm may produce a wide variety of plants. Except for root crops like radishes, carrots, and parsnips, you may grow whatever sort of plant you choose. You will fall in love with window farming as soon as you try it. It also makes a good background for selfies. So if you love photos, you've just discovered some beautiful backgrounds.

Window farming is pretty fashionable. You will not only learn proper agricultural practices, you will also be able to consume healthier, more nutritious food. Window farming does not take up much time, and the reward is healthy meals all year long.

Grow Edible Flowers

Consider fruits and vegetables that will brighten your landscape while adding color and intrigue. Swiss chard, a healthy, cold-weather crop, is a good example. It proliferates and comes in a spectrum of hues.

Basil produces a beautiful purple bloom that may be used as a garnish or added to salads. You may grow squash for its flowers if your season is not long enough for melons. Squash blossoms appear in recipes such as Squash Flower Soup. They are also a lovely, vibrant plant to have around.

SQUARE FOOT GARDENING

As the name indicates, a square-shaped farming bed is constructed. Square foot gardening is a straightforward way of growing small, well-organized, and very productive gardens. It is done by creating a 4 X 4-foot or 4 X 8-foot bed and splitting it into one-foot  squares that can be managed separately. Different seeds or seedlings are placed in each square, with the density being determined by the plant size.

To know the number of plots needed in a square foot garden, multiply the width and length of the space. For instance, if the garden is four feet on each side, you will have sixteen beds because 4 x 4 is 16. If it is a rectangular garden, the length should be multiplied by the breadth. For example, if a rectangular garden is 4 ft x 3 ft, there will be twelve beds because 4 X 3 is equal to 12

So, now that you know the basics of square foot gardening, let us look at some of the pros.

THE PROS OF SQUARE FOOT GARDENING

High Yields: Square foot gardening allows you to grow a lot of produce in a small area, making it ideal for people with small gardens.

Fast Set-up: Square foot gardening is an excellent approach for first-timers as it's a simple way to start a new garden. You can situate your raised bed almost anywhere, including on grass or concrete, and you can build, fill, and plant it in only a few hours.

Minimal Regular Maintenance: Because the garden is small, you only need to devote a few minutes to planting, maintaining, and harvesting.

Less Weeding: There will be fewer or no weeds to remove in the first season of a square foot gardening, depending on the compost used.

However, when seeds germinate, the weeds also start to grow.

COMPANION PLANTING USING SQUARE FOOT GARDENING

There are several advantages to companion planting in square foot gardening. It saves not only space but also energy. Furthermore, you may produce more vegetable kinds in a smaller space. The appropriate crop combination helps minimize weeds and pests. However, it is critical to maintain proper spacing and keep plant heights in mind for maximum production.

How to Companion Plant Within a Square Foot Garden

To companion plant within a square foot garden, make a 16 square grid from a 4 x 4-foot square. Every square foot is treated as a unique patch, with a certain number of plants planted per square foot. The same concepts used during companion planting should be used in the square foot garden. Companion pairs will be discussed in greater detail in Chapter 7.

Why Companion Planting is Essential in a Square Foot Garden

A square-foot garden is perfect even if you have ample space to nurture your plants. As I highlighted in Chapter 1, plants definitely grow better alongside each other, some more than others. Still, the results will astonish you if done right. For example, a 4 x 4 square foot garden will allow you to grow sixteen different plants, and you may even attract better insects, predators, and pollinators.

How Many Plants Can You Plant in a Square Foot Garden

It is essential to know the amount of plants you will plant. This is because if there are too many seeds in a bed or if they are planted too close together, plants tend to grow smaller. Plants, like other living things, will fight for survival. That is why knowing the amount of seed per bed is necessary.

How Do We Start

Look at every square as a place for the seeds to grow. Ensure that the seed neighbors are companion plants that do not fight for nutrition. It is essential to plant a good neighbor next to each plant. Not all plants are good neighbors. These include beans, onions, garlic, etc. This does not suggest that garlic and onions can't be grown on the same grid as beans. It simply implies that at least two squares must separate them.

Plant Spacing Cheat Sheet

Carrots need around three inches between them to grow, so you can grow up to sixteen in a square foot area. I will show you how to calculate that below.

Determining the Right Space

The following steps should be followed to determine a suitable space:

Step 1: Look for the seed spacing number on the back of your seed packet. (We will use a spacing of 3 inches for this example.)

Step 2: Divide the width of your planting portion (about 12 inches) by the 3-inch seed spacing: This gives you four plants per twelve inches.

Step 3: Repeat Step 2 above for the length of your planting area. (For example, if your planting area is twelve inches, 12 in/3 in = four plants.)

Step 4: Multiply your answers to get the total number of plants for the area, i.e., four plants on one side and four plants on the other side = sixteen plants.

Step 5: Gather your planting materials. With 3-inch seed plant spacing restrictions, you can grow sixteen plants in one square foot.

Step 6: Continue to plant. You now know how to space your plants for the rest of your garden.

HOW TO CREATE A SQUARE FOOT GARDEN

Square foot gardening has a long history in the gardening industry, with several obvious gardening and lifestyle benefits. What are the unique approaches that provide such excellent results? They are effortless and simple to master at their most basic level:

Get Your Grow Space: Firstly, build or purchase a 4-by-4-ft garden box

Put In Your Preferred Soil: Situate it in your desired location. Fill it with a nutrient-rich potting soil mix like compost, vermiculite, or any weed-free combination of your choice.

Lay Out Your Grid: Place a square foot grid onto your box for plant spacing and plant your seeds. This picture shows the square foot grid accomplished by wood being laid across. You can also use string.

Get Growing: These stages appear very straightforward, don't they? However, you may have seen the apparent difference between this system and others: the square-foot grid. The grid is usually homemade and is easy to build.

It is constructed using tiny long planks and in a way that some sets of planks are lined up vertically, and others are lined up horizontally. The grid is then used to measure and mark particular 1 x 1-ft planting spots for herbs, vegetables, and other plants.

HOW TO BUILD A RAISED BED

Raised bed gardening is a fantastic way to grow different fruits, plants, and vegetables. The advantages of raised bed gardening include a better drainage system, controlled soil temperature, and the capacity to use the best soil type for plant development.

Consider what you want to plant in your raised beds before building them. This will influence the depth and kind of soil needed, among other factors. Most people begin building a new raised bed in the winter if the soil is

not wet or frozen or in late summer when temperatures are cooler. These are the steps on how to build a raised bed:

Step 1

Decide on the size and location of your raised bed. Ensure there is enough room on both sides to stroll around without damaging your plants. Raised beds must be at least eight inches deep, but some plant species must be planted eighteen to twenty-four inches deep. Most root crops require a soil depth of twenty-four inches or more to root firmly. If you are going to build on a hard surface, make sure to provide a minimum depth of sixteen inches.

Step 2

Once a place has been selected, mark out the space, clear all weeds, and level as needed.

Step 3

Choose your materials. Maybe old scaffolding boards, railway sleepers, bricks, stone, logs, cement bricks, or plastic. Timber is cheap but short-lived, whereas sleepers are more expensive and difficult to deal with but endure far longer. Place holding posts at the corner of each raised bed. Two-inch timber posts should be buried at least twelve inches into the earth at each corner.

Step 4

To keep your raised bed walls in place, use screws or nails to fasten them to the stakes.

Step 5

It is time to add the dirt. Use high-quality top soils, such as a fertilizer-and compost-enriched mix. As you fill up the container, make sure to compress the earth with a shovel. Next, fill the frame with soil until it is level with the top. The dirt will inevitably drop as it settles.

TIP BOX

I am about to share some important tips with you. They will help you with your gardening and other life experiences.

1. Carry Out Research

Do your research before planting your seeds (or transplanting your seedlings) into your square foot garden. Learn what can be planted together in each square.

2. Not Every Plant Gets Along

Some species compete for nutrients, while others attract pests that might harm their plant neighbors. On the other hand, there are some great pairings: they attract the right insects or pollinators.

3. There is No Monoculture

Plant a variety of mutually beneficial plants in your square foot garden. However, remember that some types of plants close together can attract pests and diseases.

CONCLUSION

This chapter has been a fantastic journey, providing much information. I believe that, by now, you know the importance of preparing and planning a companion garden using raised beds and square gardening methods. You know how to pick the perfect location and plan a small garden.

You now understand the concepts of companion planting and its benefits. You know the steps required to prepare and plan for a companion garden. You also became familiar with different type of planting methods. The next chapter will look at the compost and soil requirements. It will also highlight nutrients that should always be present in your soil. In addition, it will describe ways to make homemade organic fertilizers.

COMPOST AND SOIL

L ike the foundation of a house, the soil is the foundation of any planting. It does not matter if the soil is underground or in a man-made container. Soil is an all-important team member of a successful garden. It is essential to know the contents of the ideal soil and which soil type should be in our garden. Join me on another ride as we take a tour around compost and soil.

I vividly remember that after leaving home, all I wanted was to have my own garden. I was sure I knew it all because I came from a family that practiced organic farming. Little did I know that I was deceiving myself. In my first season as a garden owner, I expected a big harvest and was shocked by my poor crop. I picked up my mobile phone and called my mom immediately. After I explained my predicament, the first question she asked me was how well I knew the soil.

She wanted to know my soil type. I was dumbfounded. I could not answer her question. Then, it dawned on me that the role of good soil cannot be overestimated. You will have a good harvest if you have good soil, but you will have a bountiful harvest if you have perfect soil. So, this chapter will talk about the ideal soil and how to make organic composts.

THE IDEAL SOIL

A perfect or ideal soil comprises 25% air, 25% water, 45% minerals, and 5% organic matter. Each component helps the plant's growth by providing crucial environmental characteristics. Plant development is restricted if any of these elements are missing from the soil. All plant cells require air to carry out the critical life function known as respiration. Any cells that do not breathe will eventually perish. Because all plant roots are made up of living cells, each cell requires oxygen to function correctly.

Water originates from the soil's pores. When soil is heavily saturated, air cannot get through, and the roots cannot develop. As a result, the plants' development is stunted, and they finally die. The water content of the soil is not the same as the water that plants may use to grow. Because soil water is firmly bonded, it can only be tested after the earth has been air-dried. Irrigation water can be added to water that is already in the soil.

Three types of soil particles make up the mineral content. They include sand, silt, and clay. The relative quantities of these elements determine the soil texture. Loam is a type of soil having equal amounts of these different components. Sandy loam is commonly thought to be an ideal soil. However, soil with a high percentage of any one particle is unsuitable for plant growth.

Organic matter makes up the last part of the soil. Organic matter is the easiest soil component to control. It retains nutrients and water efficiently. It treats a wide range of ailments in problematic soils. Waxes and tannins in organic materials in clay soils bind the microscopic clay particles into minute aggregates. This allows water to drain while also enabling air to enter the ground. The organic part of sandy soil stores water and nutrients. Organic matter enhances the soil and allows for better plant development.

Many types of organic matter are used to improve garden soils. These organic materials include commercial products, animal dung, homemade composts, and various other substances that fall into this category.

Adding a substantial quantity of organic matter to your garden soil every year promotes productive, workable soil.

Improving the Soil

One may argue that one of the most important aspects of organic gardening is enriching the soil. Feed the earth, and the plants will feed themselves. Plants that grow in healthy soil are more robust, more vigorous, and better equipped to withstand pests and disease. What does your soil need? There is only one way to be sure: Have your soil tested. The test results will reveal the pH of the soil and which nutrients are rich or scarce; this should be done every two or three years.

Adding Organic Matter

Incorporating organic material into your soil, particularly manure and natural soil supplements, is critical for your gardening success. It helps maintain a balanced pH, contributes vital minerals for plant development, and allows the ground to retain more water, which is especially beneficial if you live in the dry West.

Soil pH

The pH measures the acidity or alkalinity of your soil. The pH of the earth is particularly significant and directly impacts the availability of nutrients. The pH scale runs from zero to fourteen, with seven being the neutral value. Numbers lower than seven indicate acidity, whereas numbers higher than seven indicate alkalinity.

The quality of plant development is influenced by various environmental factors, including the pH of the soil. Plants can only absorb nutrients that are soluble in water. If the pH of the soil is too high or too low, the required substances may stay insoluble or be unable to dissolve.

Increasing Soil pH: You can apply an alkaline substance to rectify acidic soil. The term used to describe this process is liming, likely because adding limestone is the most prevalent treatment. The smaller the lime particles, the faster they become effective. Different soils will require varying amounts of lime to change the pH value.

When changing the pH value, consider the quality of the soil, the organic content, and the plants to be cultivated. To find out how much lime you will need, use the Limestone Calculator. The pH of the soil can be raised by using wood ashes. However, they degrade swiftly, so proceed with caution. An excessive application might result in a catastrophic soil imbalance.

Decreasing Soil pH: An acid supply is required to rectify alkaline soil. Organic gardeners generally tend to utilize elemental sulfur. On the other hand, sulfur takes some time to be turned into sulfuric acid by soil microorganisms. The quantity of moisture in the soil, soil temperature, and the prevalence of microorganisms influence the conversion rate. As a result, decreasing the pH value might take many months. Use the Sulfur Calculator online to figure out how much sulfur you will need. Changing the pH by more than one pH unit a year is not recommended.

BENEFITS OF HEALTHY SOIL

Having healthy soil is an advantage when planting your garden. Healthy soils have a stronger capacity to absorb and hold water, reducing evaporation and resisting dryness and severe weather conditions. The nutritional richness of foods is also improved when the soil nourishes plants rather than when synthetic fertilizers are used.

Healthy soil also helps crops combat diseases and pests, thereby decreasing the need for expensive pesticides. Since there is no need for pesticides, there is no pollution, and the water quality is improved. Below are some of the benefits of healthy soil.

Water Benefits

- Healthy soil minimizes evaporation and prevents run-off and erosion in your garden.
- Healthy soil functions like a sponge, absorbing and storing more

rainwater in your garden and replenishing groundwater and reservoirs.

- Pollutants are filtered by healthy soil, which enhances water quality.

Nutritious Food

- The nutritional value of food and forage is increased when the soil is healthy. So, you can be assured that you will be eating nutritious food.
- Plants get the nourishment they need from healthy soil, which also helps them withstand pests and diseases naturally.

Economic Security

- Your farm's production and stability are enhanced by healthy soil.
- Healthy soil requires less input, resulting in a higher-yield harvest.
- Healthy soil is more resistant to adverse weather, flooding, and drought.

Environmental and Health Benefits

- Healthy soil helps take carbon from the atmosphere, where it is released as a greenhouse gas. In this way, your garden supports microbial activity and provides a reservoir of organic N, P, and other nutrients for plant productivity.
- A healthy soil environment promotes the growth of soil microbes, which, in turn, increases nutrient levels in your garden.

- More biodiversity and species stability are supported by healthy soil, making your garden more productive.

HOW TO MAKE YOUR OWN COMPOST

Composting is an integral part of organic gardening and has several environmental advantages. While most people begin composting to find a cheaper supply of organic substances for their gardens, the benefits of composting extend well beyond the garden. Here are some of the purposes of compost:

Providing Plant Nutrients

Compost is created when soil bacteria and larger animals like earthworms ingest organic waste and break it down into a form that plants will readily absorb as nutrition. While compost contains less than four percent of any vital plant nutrients, it helps decrease or eliminate the amount of fertilizer you need.

Improving Soil Quality

Most gardeners highly value compost because of its capacity to enhance their garden soil. Organic matter should ideally make up around five percent of the soil. Compost is a fantastic supply of organic matter, but it is more than that. The majority of gardeners use it to strengthen the soil quality in their gardens, which provides protection and support for the root systems of their plants. Compost holds everything together by clumping tiny soil particles into bigger clumps that are simpler to deal with. Roots are kept oxygenated by air spaces between soil mineral particles, and compost improves this oxygenation.

Compost is the soil that helps the garden retain enough water to keep plants from drying out while allowing excess water to flow away. This enhanced nutrient retention is aided by improved hydration retention. Compost increases the number of helpful bacteria in the soil, which drives out disease-causing microbes.

Reducing Waste

Many individuals want to limit the quantity of trash they throw out each week. The typical American generates over four pounds of garbage every day. Composting is one way to lessen this. Food scraps, paper, eggshells, cotton and wool towels, pet hair, and autumn leaves are just a few examples of things that can be turned into compost instead of being thrown out.

Saving Money

Gardeners may save money by turning garbage into plant nutrients instead of buying compost, cattle manure, and other organic resources to enhance their soil. Compost provides a steady supply of nutrients throughout the growing season, eliminating the need for frequent fertilizer treatments to keep plants healthy.

What is the Purpose of Composting?

Composting is the process of converting natural materials into a product that improves soil quality. As an alternative to those expensive chemically enriched fertilizers, anyone can manufacture compost at home at a low cost. Apart from that, much consumer trash is also recycled through composting.

What to Compost?

Nitrogen-rich materials degrade fast. So, grass clippings, leaves, and other nitrogen-rich materials like hay, pine straw, and weeds degrade fast, making them easy to compost. In addition to that, untreated sawdust and other garden wastes all fall into the category of what to compost. Kitchen trash like eggshells, tea bags, ground coffee, and vegetable and fruit peels can all be composted.

What not to Compost?

Chemically treated wood products such as sawdust, human or animal wastes, bones, meat, oily food wastes, and poisonous weeds should not be composted. Find out where sawdust came from before adding it to a compost pile. An infection may spread through diseased plants, human waste, and pet waste. In addition, meat, bones, and oily food waste take a long time to break down, attracting pests and flies.

Composting Essentials

Compost piles require fresh air to break down since composting is aerobic. It is important to know that covered or sealed compost mounds do not decompose. It is simpler for bacteria to spread when a compost pile is wet, so keep your pile moist. Also, compost piles in cold weather do not work as quickly as during warm weather as they do not decompose well in the cold.

Completed Compost

A compost pile is ready for fertilizing soil when it develops a dark brown color and smells like damp soil or dirt. You can also use your compost before it finishes decaying; it will continue to decompose while feeding the soil. Never use compost that has gone bad or rotten.

Uses of Compost

Compost can be used as a cover by gardeners to protect plant roots. It is also utilized to improve soil, mixed with soil in pot mixes or made into compost tea, a liquid fertilizer sprayed onto plants and crops.

Steps for Making Your Own Compost Cheap at Home

Autumn is the best time to start composting. You have plenty of farm waste from trimming your garden and other environmentally friendly waste mentioned above. Follow these ten easy steps to make your own compost heap at home. It's fun, so enjoy!

1. Container

Choose a container for composting and place it in a grassy, shaded area of your garden. Ensure the container has no bottom and the compost heap is directly on the ground. Also make sure that it is the proper size for you and your household. It should have enough room to hold everything you need to get rid of, but it should not be too big.

2. Base

Put a few layers of leaves and sticks at the bottom to aerate the pile.

3. Balance

An appropriate balance of nitrogen, water, carbon, and air is required for successful composting. The green elements you utilize will have nitrogen, while the brown stuff will have carbon.

4. Preparation

Before putting any large lumps of stuff in the container, cut or split them up.

5. Include

To have successful compost, include any of the following: fruits, dried leaves, grass clippings, tea leaves, used pet bedding, dry dog or cat food, dust from vacuuming or sweeping, shredded newspaper, human and pet hair, wine corks, manure, coffee grounds, and other eco-friendly things should make the list.

6. Avoid

Avoid anything that will attract pests, like bread and dairy foods. Also, avoid highly processed foods that take longer to decompose.

7. Bury

If you regularly add to the compost heap, it is advisable to bury the new bits beneath the pile that is already starting to decompose rather than just putting them on top.

8. Aerate

The pile should be aerated at least once a week using a shovel or spade.

9. Water

If you think the pile is becoming too dry, dampen it with water. If it is a scorching day, you might want to cover your pile to keep it wet.

10. Ready to use

After a few months, your compost should be ready to use. The compost is ready when you notice it turning a dark brown color, developing an unpleasant smell, and becoming warm when you touch it. This is due to the bacteria living in it.

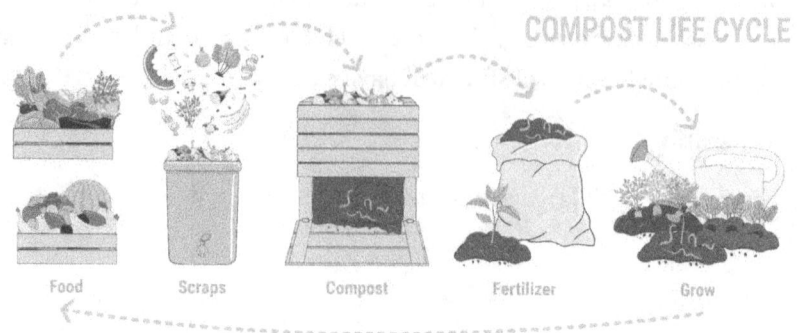

COMPOST LIFE CYCLE

Food   Scraps   Compost   Fertilizer   Grow

Using Organic Fertilizers

It can be easy to become overwhelmed when deciding what to feed your plants. When you consider the many kinds of fertilizers, the condition of your soil, and the specific requirements of your unique plants, it might be tempting to forgo the whole thing. However, if you don't fertilize your plants, they will not develop or flourish as you would like them to. In addition to sunshine and water, plants require specific nutrients to grow, and if you do not refill their supply regularly, they may develop health problems.

Why Plants Need Fertilizer

Like you and I, plants require certain nutrients to thrive and grow. They need a lot of nitrogen, phosphorus, and potassium, known as macronutrients. (Other micronutrients are needed in such small amounts that you do not have to bother about them.) You will ultimately end up with unhappy plants with fragile branches, smaller leaves, fewer blooms, and poor color if they don't get enough of these macronutrients.

The good news is that fertilizer can fix most nutritional shortages, whether your plants grow in a garden or a container.

Why You Need to Test Your Soil before Adding Fertilizer

Although it may seem that your plants are absorbing all their nutrients from your garden soil, this is not always the case. The nutrient levels in your soil may be inadequate and influenced by where you live and what has previously been growing there. In the case of newer homes, dirt added after building may result in inferior soil deficient in organic matter, which is the primary natural source of nutrients. Even if you have rich soil, this may have become depleted over time.

Therefore, you first need to determine the nutritional condition of your garden before applying fertilizer. The best way to do this is by testing the soil. Otherwise, you risk squandering money on fertilizer that you do not need or hurting your plants by using too much or the wrong fertilizer. Imagine a situation where you spend money buying medication for pneumonia instead of for malaria because you failed to run a test. You can imagine how expensive and disastrous that would be.

Your soil test findings will generally tell you how much of each nutrient you require. It is also a good idea to run a soil test every year because plants use different quantities each year. At least you know your garden soil is improving *nutritiously*.

Four Steps to Test for Soil pH

The soil test is a kit that indicates your soil pH level. Your soil pH level determines how well your plants can absorb nutrients and thrive. Typically, soil pH level ranges from 1.0 to 14.0, indicating highly acidic to highly alkaline conditions, with seven considered neutral. To test for soil pH in your garden, follow these steps:

1. Collect Soil

To start, use a trowel to collect soil particles from at least six different locations in your garden. Make sure you dig a minimum of six inches down in each place when collecting your soil samples, ensuring no roots, debris, or pebbles are collected. Approximately one teaspoon of dirt from each spot is required.

2. Mix Samples

Mix a small number of soil particles from each spot in a quart jar or another clean, similar-size container to produce an average soil sample of a large area. Use a trowel to break up any big clumps.

Note: Avoid touching the samples taken with your bare hands. The oils on your fingertips might change the soil's pH equilibrium, influencing your soil test results.

3. Combine Soil and Testing Powder

Fill the soil test kit vial with your soil sample using a spoon. Only a small soil sample is required, just enough to fill the hole to the designated line. Next, take one of the soil test kit's capsules and gently open it. Fill the soil test vial halfway with powder.

4. Add Water

Add water to your soil specimen vial using the plastic eyedropper included in your test kit. To test your soil, use distilled water; water-containing additives might also influence your findings. Pour water into the soil test vial until the dotted line is reached. Cover the test kit vial and shake it vigorously to mix the soil, water, and testing powder.

Allow one to two minutes for the liquid in your shaken vial to settle and form a color before assessing the results. The color of the liquid will determine the pH level of your soil (see the instructions included with your soil test equipment). Then, bring your vial up to the light or sun for the best color assessment.

Garden Fertilizers: The Best Homemade Natural Fertilizers

Many natural garden fertilizers may be used with your pot soil. Some fertilizers can be made at home with a standard kitchen or backyard materials. Below are eight of our favorite homemade fertilizers that can be used for various applications.

1. Grass Clippings

Grass clippings are an excellent source of nitrogen. If you have organic grass, save the grass clippings and lay them in your garden. Grass clippings may also be made into compost.

2. Weeds

Weed tea is a fantastic fertilizer. Many of the weeds in your garden, including grass clippings, are high in nitrogen and make excellent fertilizers. The trouble is that once you have picked the weeds out of the garden, you do not want to bring them back since any seeds will grow and create more weeds. So, what would you do?

Prepare weed tea. Fill ¼ of a five-gallon bucket with the weeds you have pulled out. Then fill the bucket with water and soak the weeds for a week or two. Pour this nutritionally rich weed tea over your gardens once the water has become brown (like tea).

3. Kitchen Scraps

Make your compost from your kitchen and yard garbage. Compost does take a long time to release nutrients, so a well-composted garden may last a year or two without fertilizer. Compost aids in retaining moisture in the soil, which is necessary for vegetable plants to thrive in the hot, dry summer months.

4. Manure

Cows, horses, poultry, and even bats contribute to manure production. Although each type of manure is abundant in nitrogen and other nutrients, use it with caution. Because raw manure is very acidic and may contain more nutrients than your plants can absorb, too much might cause your plants to burn. It is recommended to use compost manure. You may use more to boost your soil's water retention without endangering your plants because it is less nutritious and acidic. You won't have to wait long because manure quickly decomposes into an odor-free soil additive.

5. Tree Leaves

Instead of bagging up your fall leaves and tossing them on the curb, gather them up for your gardening. Leaves are high in essential minerals that attract earthworms, retain water, and benefit heavy soils. You may either

plow leaves into your ground (you can add crushed leaves to your potting soil) or use them as a cover to nurture your plants while keeping weeds at bay.

6. Ground Coffee

One of the finest applications for coffee grinds is as a plant fertilizer. Many plants flourish in acidic soil, including blueberries, rhododendrons, roses, and tomatoes. Recycle your coffee grinds to help your soil become more acidic. You may top-feed your soil by scattering the used grinds over the soil's surface, or you can prepare "coffee" to sprinkle on your plants. To prepare garden coffee, ferment up to six cups of old coffee grounds in water for up to a week before using them to water acid-loving plants.

7. Eggshells

Eggshells might help your soil become less acidic. Have you ever used lime in your garden? If so, you will be aware that it has several advantages, like reducing the acid level of your soil for those plants that prefer a more alkaline environment and providing plants with large amounts of calcium, which is a necessary nutrient.

Lime is a natural fertilizer available at your local garden shop, but there is a less expensive way to achieve the same results. Simply clean your kitchen eggshells and grind them for use in your garden. Eggshells consist of ninety-three percent calcium carbonate, the chemical term for lime.

8. Banana Peels

Bananas and roses are high in potassium. Simply bury the banana peels near the rose bushes to allow them to compost organically. Then, bury the peels in the top layer of soil as the roses grow. This method will give the plant the potassium it requires for optimum development.

CONCLUSION

If you have followed me on this ride, you should now know the components of ideal soil. You should also know how to make your own compost and fertilizers. I have shown you different methods to do this. Whichever approach you find most convenient, trust me when I say you will not regret it. Just make sure you test the soil's pH level before applying compost and fertilizers.

Of course, you know that plants' basic needs are sunlight, water, and air. In the next chapter, we will be looking at watering and the light requirements for your garden. So let's jump on this moving train and look at this topic.

TEST YOUR KNOWLEDGE

Test your knowledge with the following five questions. Answer them before checking the answers.

1. Which of the following should not be composted?

    a. Banana peels
    b. Egg shells
    c. Dairy products

2. What percentage of mineral matter should be present in an ideal soil?

    a. Twenty-five percent (25%)
    b. Forty-five percent (45%)
    c. Five percent (5%)

3. Which of these methods can be used to raise the soil's pH level?

    a. Sulphur
    b. Kitchen waste
    c. Wood ashes

4. When running a pH test, what does a level of six indicate?

    a. The soil is acidic
    b. There is alkalinity in the soil
    c. The soil is neutral

5. How many soil samples should you take when you want to run a pH test on your garden soil?

    a. At least six

b. At least five

c. At least three

Answers

1. c
2. b
3. c
4. a
5. a

4

WATER AND LIGHT REQUIREMENTS

I must commend you for coming this far with me. Although we are not there yet, we have come a long way. In this episode of companion planting, we will take an in-depth look at water and light as essential requirements for a good garden. Then, we will expand on the rules of watering, lighting, and many more.

When I was starting my vegetable garden, I chanced upon my niece. She had just finished reading my notes on "things to consider before gardening." She informed me she had something to share.

"Hey, young woman, I am all ears."

She jumped down from the chair, stood in front of me like a woman who wanted to read a presidential manifesto, looked at my face, and cleared her throat.

"Dear Mrs. Bird," she started, "you should consider the light and water before deciding which vegetables to plant."

I looked at her with an expression that said, "I know, young one."

She continued, "How do you think nutrients travel through the plant? Water! Yes, water does the trick. How do plants make food using photosynthesis? Light! Yes, light is what you need. So let us consider a spot with the right amount of light and water. Since we do not want too much water, I suggest *that* spot," she concluded.

I looked at the spot she was pointing to, where I had intended to locate my vegetable garden. I stood up, hugged her, and gave her an agreeing nod. "You are becoming a better gardener than I am!" was all I could say.

DETERMINING WATER NEEDS

Many people do wonder how much water they should give their garden. They also wonder what time they should water their garden. It is not that hard, but some factors should be considered when watering a garden.

When to Water Your Garden?

It is believed that about one or two inches of water for deep watering weekly or regular shallow watering is ideal. However, these two approaches depend on factors such as:

Soil

Consider your soil first. Sandy soil will store less water than clay soil, which is heavier. As a result, it will dry up faster, but the clay-like soil will retain moisture for a longer period (and is more likely to be harmed by overwatering). This is why adding compost to the earth is so crucial. A healthier soil not only drains better but also promotes some water retention. Mulch can also help you save money on water by reducing the amount of water you need to use.

Weather

The weather also determines how much and how often to water garden plants. If it is hot and dry outside, you will need to water it more frequently. Naturally, minimal watering is required when it rains.

Plants

Plants, too, have a say in when and how frequently they are watered. Different plants require different amounts of watering, with bigger and newly planted ones requiring more water. In addition, vegetables and many perennials have shallower root systems, which necessitates more regular watering, sometimes even daily, especially in temperatures above 85 º F.

Time of Day

Most container plants requires regular watering in hot, dry weather, often twice or thrice a day. When it comes to watering gardens, the time of day is equally important. Morning watering is best since it lowers evaporation, but late afternoon watering is fine as long as you do not get the foliage wet, which might cause fungal problems.

How Much Water to Give Plants?

Ideally, gardens should receive around one inch of water per week.

The Benefits of Deep Watering

Watering more frequently but not deeply results in lower root development and higher evaporation. Except for lawns, which lose less water to evaporation, overhead sprinklers are generally frowned upon. Soaker hoses or drip watering are usually preferred since they reach the roots directly while keeping the foliage dry.

Deep watering fosters root development that is both deeper and stronger. However, hand watering is best reserved for smaller garden spaces and container plants due to its time commitment.

THE TEN GOLDEN RULES OF WATERING

Here are some helpful and smart rules for watering your plants.

Rule 1: Maintain good moisture levels. The majority of plants rely on consistent wetness. However, allowing the plants to dry out a little before watering encourages root development.

Rule 2: Water less often but thoroughly. One to two weekly watering sessions are typically adequate in flower beds: it is preferable to water infrequently but thoroughly than to water frequently but not enough.

Rule 3: Water in the late evening or early in the morning. Less water evaporates when you water the soil in the evening or at night. Plants will be able to replenish their water supplies before the heat settles in the next day.

Rule 4: Keep the leaves dry. Wet leaves rot and get infected. Leaves exposed to the sun get damp and create tiny burn scars. Leaf-mold illnesses can occur if they are kept moist overnight.

Rule 5: Water must reach the root. Appropriate watering ensures that enough water reaches the roots. Water volumes that are too low but frequent just cover the top layer of the soil. Adequate irrigation is therefore essential.

Rule 6: Apply gradually. It takes a few moments for the water to permeate into the soil, and it is preferable to water the bed in sections rather than letting the valuable water flow away unused.

Rule 7: Water evenly around the plant. Watering only one root point causes one-sided root development and, as a result, inadequate nutrient retention in the soil. As a result, water the plants' surroundings and the irrigation area.

Rule 8: Use water-saving irrigation methods. This is made easier by installing an auto-irrigation system with a moisture sensor on the bed, balcony, and grass.

Rule 9: Avoid waterlogging. Waterlogging prevents the roots from breathing air from the soil, causing the root cells to drown.

Rule 10: Use quality clay-rich soil for better water retention. Soil rich in clay minerals has excellent expansion qualities, which allows it to retain water better and more evenly. To avoid waterlogging during rainy summers and winters, provide proper drainage.

METHODS OF WATERING

Depending on the type of garden you have, how much you can spend, and how much time have, here are some methods of watering:

Watering Can

A watering can is ideal for watering a few potted plants or freshly planted seeds that only require a little sprinkling.

+ PROS

Because a watering can is so portable, you can use it to get water to any part of your property and even where the hose will not reach.

– CONS

When filled, big cans are heavy and difficult to carry.

It is good to water plants softly (rather than thoroughly) so that you do not have to return to the tap as often. Unfortunately, this causes plants to have shallow root systems, requiring more frequent watering and thus limiting their growth potential.

Garden Hose with Nozzle

A garden hose with a nozzle may be used to irrigate various types of vegetation, including pots, raised beds, plants, and even tiny lawns.

Choose a nozzle that offers at least two spray options: jet and shower. A jet setting is ideal for cleaning pots and birdbaths and watering shrubs that the hose cannot touch, while a shower setting is ideal for watering matured plants. You may use a hose wand for extended reach, although it generally only has one setting (a gentle spray).

+ PROS

Hoses and nozzles are affordable and readily available and may be used to water almost any type of garden.

− CONS

You will have to lift and move the hose around to water every plant.

Sprinklers

Sprinklers are cheap and come in various forms, including the famous oscillating sprinkler, which waters by rotating in a semi-circle. Water-saving, multi-pattern sprinklers allow you to tailor the spray to your garden's size and form. Sprinklers may be used to irrigate raised bed gardens, landscaping plants, lawns, and vegetable gardens, among other things.

+ PROS

Sprinklers provide moderate watering that saturates freshly planted seedbeds while also producing an overhead shower that repels pests and creepy crawlies.

When not watering the garden, use the sprinkler to cool yourself down.

− CONS

The sprinkler must be carried to every area that requires watering. The site nearest to the sprinkler usually receives more water than areas further away, and you are likely to lose a significant amount of water due to the wind drift.

When there is a lot of humidity, leaves might stay damp even after being watered, promoting disease growth.

Soaker Hoses

A soaker hose, sometimes known as a leaky hose, is placed between plants in the soil and "sweats" water along its whole length. There is far less waste than overhead watering since the water gets straight into the ground. With tightly spaced plantings and raised bed gardens, a soaker hose is an ideal option.

+ PROS

By distributing water directly to the earth, soaker hoses conserve water. Because plant leaves are not damp, illness is less likely to spread.

− CONS

Unless you buy a timer, you will have to leave the water flowing for an extended period to soak the ground thoroughly enough for optimal growth.

Drip Irrigation

Water is supplied directly to the soil through emitters in a drip irrigation system. Slow yet continuous streams of water are discharged, gradually wetting each plant's root zone. Some drip irrigation systems include a snip-and-drip option that allows you to tailor the location of the water delivery tubes. Drip irrigation is perfect for container gardening, raised bed gardens, and planting beds.

+ PROS

Drip irrigation uses a lot less water than other types of irrigation.

It offers a hands-free method of watering plants and may be readily automated with a timer.

— CONS

If your garden is not level, water flow and distribution may be inconsistent.

As rodents try to get to the water, holes in drip tubes and nozzles can get clogged with silt and material build-up from hard water and may entice rodents to chew and destroy lines.

Water Sensors and Controllers

Water sensors detect how dry the soil is and notify you when it is time to water. When your plants are thirsty, the water sensor starter kit sends a notification to your phone or tablet. Smart water controllers go even farther, activating your in-ground irrigation system to water your plants when the soil becomes dry.

The controller optimizes the watering schedule automatically depending on local, real-time meteorological data. Controllers operate well with irrigation systems for lawns, raised gardens, and landscaping areas, whereas sensors may be installed anywhere.

+ PROS

This type of technology-based watering saves water by only supplying what plants require when they require it.

It is also super-easy to use, allowing you to accomplish the entire task from your preferred mobile device, no matter where you are.

− CONS

Covering all parts of your garden may need many sensors, and the original investment might be expensive.

CONSERVING WATER

Follow these simple guidelines to conserve water while keeping your plants healthy and happy:

Improve Soil and Use Compost

Add organic materials like compost, chopped leaves, or composted manure to enrich your soil. These organic compounds improve the soil's water-holding capacity. A good rule of thumb is to add one inch of compost every year. The compost will help the ground retain water for extended periods without becoming saturated.

Add Mulch

Spread mulch over the ground. Mulch keeps weeds from sprouting and absorbs the water you pour over the planting area. The best value for your money comes from a mulch layer; it is recommended to use organic mulch. Over time, weed-free grass clippings, evergreen needles, shredded bark, and autumn leaves will contribute nutrients to the soil.

When plants are watered, moisture immediately evaporates from the soil's surface. By adding a layer of mulch to your garden, you save water by reducing the amount of water lost via evaporation. Mulching also helps keep the soil wet for extended periods while also keeping the temperature of the earth lower in the summer and warmer in the winter.

Save Rainwater

When it rains, channel the water toward your plants rather than letting it run off. Make an additional effort to save money by collecting as much free water as possible. Install rain buckets or a reservoir at your downspouts. A 1,000-square-foot roof accumulates around 625 gallons of water from a single inch of rain. Rain gardens may also be used to collect and store rainfall.

Group Plants with Similar Watering Requirements Together

Know the features of your planting location, such as how much light and shade your garden gets, the soil type, and the wind conditions. Situate plants with similar requirements together, for example, drought-tolerant flowers. Another drought-resistant suggestion is to plant close to the home, where flowers and vegetables can be quickly irrigated. Drought-tolerant plants should be clustered at the garden's edge.

Use Indigenous Plants Where Possible

Because some plants collect all their water from rain, they require less maintenance once they have established themselves. If you're looking for drought-resistant perennials, indigenous plants that match your soil type are usually your best choice. Indigenous plants have adapted to cope with little rainfall.

They may require more water during droughts, although not as much as plants that are not acclimated to your local environment. Indigenous plants are also more pest-resistant, use less fertilizer, and require less upkeep than non-indigenous plants. If you choose to include non-indigenous plants in your garden, be sure they are well-suited to your area and do not require excessive watering.

Remove the Competition

Maintain a regular schedule for garden maintenance. Plants that are in good health require minimal maintenance. When you keep up with operations like weeding, thinning, and pruning, you improve the health of your plants, and, as a result, you will need to water them less frequently.

Allow Grass to Grow Longer

Allowing your grass to reach a height of three inches will provide shade for the roots. This helps to preserve water by reducing evaporation. Furthermore, a greater mowing height will prevent weed growth.

Reduce the Amount of Grass on Your Terrain

Grass consumes a lot of water, about fifty-five inches per year on average. Perennial-filled beds use far less water and add a pleasant splash of color to the landscape. There are various ways to produce a beautiful garden that requires little to no water if you want to remove part of, or perhaps all, your lawn.

Use Porous Landscape Materials Instead of Concrete

If you want to save water, stay away from concrete. Rainwater can infiltrate through porous surfaces like gravel or sand-set stepping stones, soaking the plants nearby.

THINK ABOUT LIGHT

Let's be practical here. Take a deep breath. Picture your garden. Think about how much sunlight it gets. Think about the direction of the sunlight. Think about the number of hours of daylight it receives each day.

I understand that not all gardens can face south and have no tall buildings or big trees to block the sunlight. But, sometimes, you just have to use what you get and hope it meets the necessary requirements.

Sunlight Requirements for Vegetables

As most people know, light is one of the basic needs for growing vegetables. Take some time to figure out when to plant and how much light you need to grow your own vegetables. Different vegetables require different levels of sunlight.

Most Vegetables Need an Average of Six Hours of Sunlight Per Day.

Some root and leaf crops thrive in shadier parts of the garden. Decide whether to put them in the front, side, or back of your house to ensure that they receive adequate sunlight, such as the morning and afternoon sun. If your potted plants receive too much or too little light each day, you can easily move them.

Vegetables that grow well in shadier areas include:

- Swiss Chard
- Lettuce
- Kale
- Peas

Fruiting vegetables that require eight hours of sunlight a day include:

- Potatoes
- Strawberries
- Cucumbers
- Peppers
- Chili
- Tomatoes
- Aubergine
- Squash

Root vegetables that require six hours of sun a day include:

- Potatoes
- Spinach
- Carrots
- Strawberries
- Radishes
- Beets

Leafy vegetables that require four hours of sunlight a day include:

- Peas
- Broccoli
- Garlic
- Cabbage
- Collard
- Lettuce
- Cauliflower
- Swiss Chard
- Asparagus
- Kale
- Spinach

Based on the information above, I would encourage you to plan your vegetable garden based on how much sunlight the vegetables require. Let the type of garden determine the kind of vegetables you will grow. For example, if you have a shady garden and want a high-yield vegetable, I recommend focusing on spinach, kale, peas, etc.

You are the architect of your garden. Gather your drawing materials because we are about to plan for sun and water in your garden together. Done? Now, follow these steps:

- Do a rough sketch of your garden on your drawing paper
- Mark out the areas with the most sun and shade
- List the vegetables that will grow in each area
- Think about watering and which type of watering method will fit your garden
- Check your budget
- Now, plan your garden according to the available funds and resources

CONCLUSION

We have been able to look at the concepts of watering and the rules of watering. We have also discussed how to conserve and water our plants. This is a significant step forward in our gardening journey.

Sunlight is also an essential factor when planning your garden. This includes the sun's direction and daily amount of sunlight. The next chapter will show you how to control and manage pests and diseases. It will also describe the likely pests in your vegetable garden. You do not want to miss it. See you in Chapter 5.

5

PEST AND DISEASE MANAGEMENT

"Worldwide, insect pests consume up to 20% of the plants that humans grow for food, and this causes farmers to use more pesticides, which could cause further environmental harm."

— KENDRA PIERRE-LOUIS

I n this chapter, you will learn about the different pests and diseases that can appear in your vegetable garden and the detrimental effects they may have on your crop. This chapter will also offer natural solutions to mitigate this problem. Are you ready? Join the moving train.

IMPACT OF PESTICIDES ON OUR HEALTH

Pesticides are poisons, and they can affect more than just the "pests" they are designed to kill. They are toxic and can harm your health in a variety of ways. They have been associated with various dangerous illnesses and disorders, ranging from asthma to cancer.

It is almost inevitable that there are pests in our gardens, and pesticides were originally designed to kill them. But do we sacrifice our health for pests? Of course not! That is why I always tell anyone who cares to listen to always use natural alternatives. There are better and more effective alternatives to pesticides. Using natural and organic options will benefit not only our health but also that of our plants.

The Importance of Being Able to Identify Pests

It is vital to be able to identify pests before taking any action against them. On the one hand, you do not want to remove a helpful bug, but on the other, you do not wish to allow a harmful pest to run riot in your garden.

The Importance of Knowing Which Pests are Most Common in Your Area

The type of pests in your garden will be determined by your location and the type of plants. For instance, a garden in Arizona will have pests specific to that area; they are different from those in California. You must be aware of the common pests in your area to be able to deal with them.

FIFTEEN COMMON PESTS TO WATCH OUT FOR

Below are some common pests to look out for in your garden:

APHIDS

Aphids can be found in tiny groups on different vegetable plants, like lettuce and cabbage.

Identification: Aphids are tiny pear-shaped insects. They can be yellow, green, brown, red, or black. Depending on their species and life stage, they can be both winged and non-winged.

Plants affected: Aphids feed on vegetable plants like tomatoes, kale, lettuce, and cabbage. They are mentioned in every garden pest guide, and their profusion makes them a common issue in most gardens.

Description of damage: Aphids suck plant juices, causing distortion and malformed growth. They usually feed in huge numbers on new plant growth or the undersides of leaves.

Preventative measures: Invite beneficial predatory insects by including a lot of companion flowering plants with small flowers in the garden.

Physical controls: Spraying aphids off plants with a sharp stream of water from the hose will kill them. Aphids may easily be squished by hand, or plants can be protected from insects using a floating row cover.

ASPARAGUS BEETLE

Asparagus beetle adults are very distinctive.

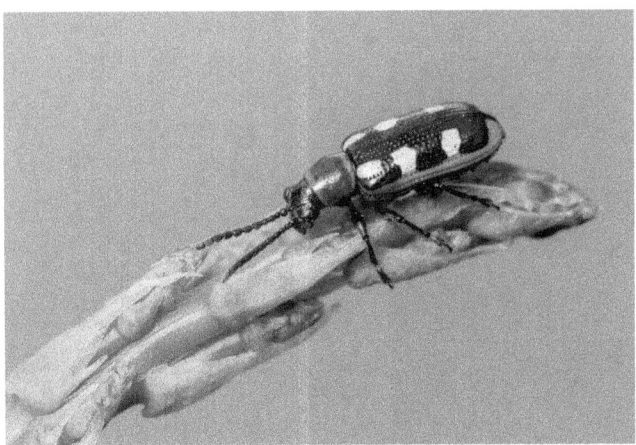

Identification: Adult asparagus beetles measure about a quarter of an inch. They have a black body with creamy yellow dots and a red patch behind their head. The larvae have a black head and are army-green in color.

Plants affected: They only feed on asparagus plants.

Description of damage: Both larvae and adults consume asparagus spears and ferns. Severe outbreaks can result in the complete browning of the leaves and a loss of the crop's vitality the following year.

Preventative measures: In the autumn, trim down ferns and tidy up fallen leaves in the asparagus patch to prevent adult asparagus beetles from overwintering in garden detritus.

Physical controls: Use a floating row cover to protect developing spears and keep them in place during the harvesting season. Squish the small, black eggs found on spears with your hands. Then, using a soft brush, remove the larvae off the plants regularly; spiders and other helpful insects will discover and devour them once on the ground.

CABBAGE WORMS

Imported cabbageworm caterpillars are very destructive in the vegetable garden.

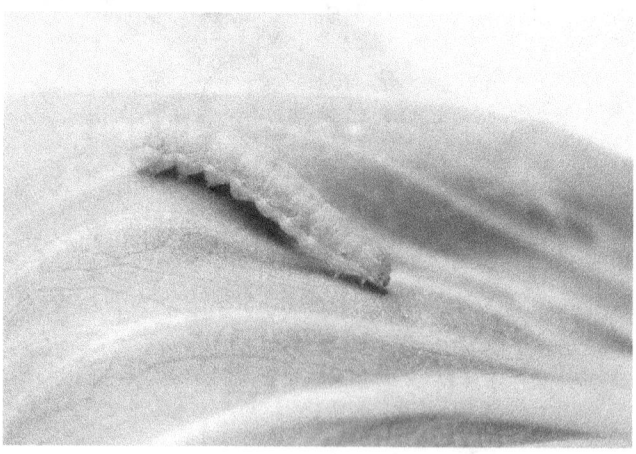

Identification: The caterpillars of imported cabbage worms are one inch long and pale green with a slight yellow stripe along their back. Adult butterflies have white to yellowish-white wings with up to four black markings.

Plants affected: Cabbage worms can be found in all members of the cabbage family, including cauliflower, cabbage, broccoli, kale, radish, turnip, kohlrabi, and brussels sprouts.

Description of damage: Cabbage worm caterpillars eat leaves and flower clusters, chewing holes in them. If the infestation is significant, it can cause complete defoliation.

Preventative measures: Birds adore eating cabbage worms, so hang birdhouses in the garden.

Physical controls: As host plants do not need to be pollinated to be productive, cover vulnerable plants with a floating crop cover from planting until harvest. Handpicking caterpillars is also a viable option.

CARROT RUST FLY

As they eat, carrot rust fly larvae leave characteristic tunnels behind.

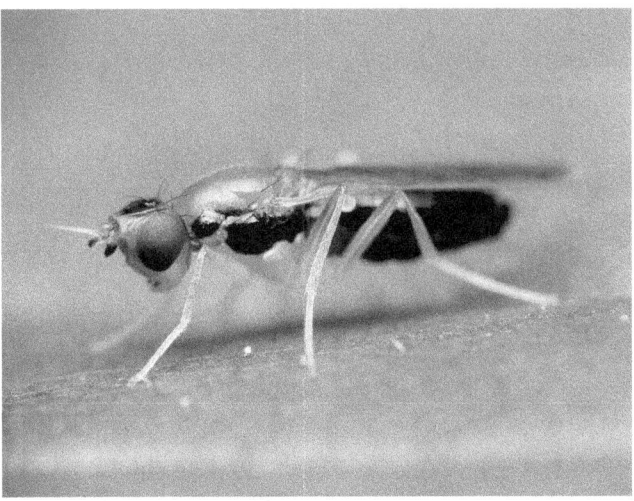

Identification: Adult carrot rust flies are tiny black flies with orange heads and legs. The larvae are small maggots with a beige tint. Though this insect does not appear in every guide on vegetable garden pests, it is becoming increasingly bothersome for many gardeners and needs to be highlighted.

Plants affected: Adult flies lay eggs near a wide range of vegetable crops, including carrots, parsley, celery, parsnips, and other root vegetables.

Description of damage: The larvae of carrot rust flies feed on crop roots, leaving behind tunnels and scars. The damage becomes increasingly visible as the season passes. As a result, the roots are riddled with tunnels and scars.

Preventative measures: Adult carrot rust flies are poor flyers; therefore, rotate crops every season as a preventative strategy. Position the crop in a different direction from last year's crop.

Physical controls: Keep carrots and other sensitive crops covered with a floating row cover from planting until harvesting. Carrots and other crops should be inter-planted with onions, garlic, and chives to help minimize carrot rust and fly egg production.

COLORADO POTATO BEETLE

The larvae of the Colorado potato beetle feed on potatoes, tomatoes, and other garden plants.

Identification: Adult Colorado potato beetles have black and tan striped wing coverings and are about 1/3 inch long. The larvae are 1/2 inch long, reddish-purple in color, and have rows of black spots on the sides.

Plants affected: Possible hosts include all members of the tomato family, like potatoes, peppers, eggplants, tomatillos, and tomatoes.

Description of damage: Damage by both adults and larvae has been described. Colorado potato bugs skeletonize the leaves right down to the veins. They are usually located near the plant's summit.

Preventative measures: Adult beetles survive the winter in garden trash, so clean up after yourself and rotate your crops every year as a preventative step.

Physical controls: Place a floating row cover over the plants and leave it in place until harvest. You may also remove the adults and larvae by hand.

CUCUMBER BEETLES

Cucumber beetles may have black stripes or black dots.

Identification: Adult cucumber beetles are around 1/4 inch long when fully grown. They have brilliant black or yellow dots or stripes, depending on the species. Their larvae are barely visible since they reside underground.

Plants affected: All members of the cucumber family, including melons, cucumbers, pumpkins, gourds, and squash, are hosts. Cucumber beetles have also been found on maize, beets, beans, and other plants.

Description of damage: Adult beetles cause bacterial wilt by leaving tiny, ragged holes on leaves and flowers.

Preventative measures: Plant cucumber beetle-resistant varieties or plant bacterial wilt-resistant cultivars like Saladin and Gemini cucumbers, butternut-type squashes, muskmelons, and squashes in the species group Cucurbita moschata, as they are less liked by the beetles.

Physical controls: Cucumber beetles may be kept off the plants by covering them with floating row cover, much like many other insects included in our guide to vegetable garden pests. However, you will need to remove the cover when the plants blossom to allow for pollination. Mulch sensitive crops with loose materials like straw or hay to prevent the laying of eggs.

CUTWORMS

Cutworms eat plant stems at ground level.

Identification: Adult cutworms are night-flying moths that are brown or gray. When disturbed, their larval caterpillars can grow up to two inches long and coil into a tight C shape. Caterpillars can be brown, yellow, green, or gray, depending on the species, and they live in the first few inches of soil.

Plants affected: Any new seedling is vulnerable, but cabbage, tomatoes, kale, broccoli, and other vegetables are favorites.

Description of damage: Cutworms tear seedlings at ground level or girdle them by nibbling the outer stem tissue, causing harm. The damage is easily identified by the wilted or damaged seedlings.

Preventative measures: Crop rotation is essential. Shelter young seedling stems at their bottom with a collar constructed device from a toilet roll tube, or aluminum foil pushed half an inch into the ground. It is also good to till the garden in the fall to expose larvae to predators and freezing weather.

Physical controls: Cutworms are drawn to cornmeal or wheat bran placed in deep basins near vulnerable plants; the caterpillars cannot digest the granules and perish.

FLEA BEETLES

Although flea beetles are small, they can wreak havoc on eggplant, radishes, and other vegetable crops.

Identification: Flea beetles are tiny black or brown bugs 1/10-inch long. They bounce about like fleas and move swiftly.

Plants affected: Flea beetles feed on a wide variety of plants, but radishes, potatoes, tomatoes, brassicas, maize, and eggplants are among their favorites.

Description of damage: Flea bugs eat plant leaves and leave tiny circular holes in them. The larvae of these insects reside below ground and can eat plant roots.

Preventative measures: Rotate your crops.

Physical controls: Place yellow sticky cards above plant tops to attract and catch adult flea beetles. A floating row cover should not be used since it can trap freshly emerging flea beetles beneath it.

LEAFMINERS

Leafminers wreak havoc on the environment by destroying the leaves of vegetables, for example, beet leaves.

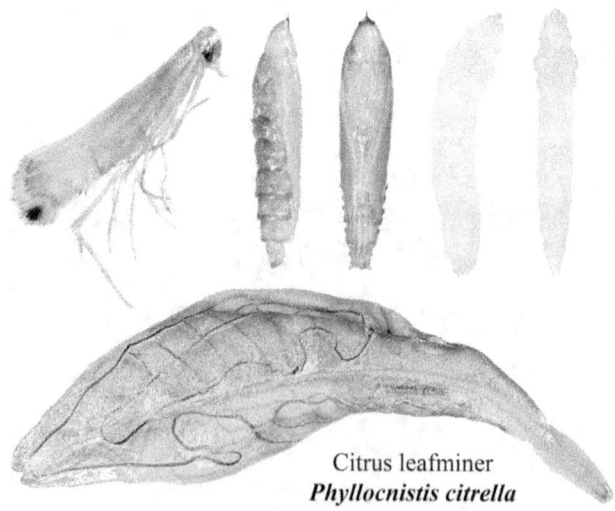

Citrus leafminer
Phyllocnistis citrella

Identification: Adult leafminers are small, inconspicuous insects that do not eat plants. Their larvae, however, which are brown or green, feed on plant tissues.

Plants affected: Leafminers feed on plants like chard, spinach, nasturtiums, beets, and blueberries.

Description of damage: Leafminer larvae crawl through layers of leaf tissue, leaving behind telltale squiggly tunnels and lines.

Preventative measures: To prevent a new generation, cut off leaves where tunnels are present during the growing season and discard them in the garbage. The damage is rarely severe enough to destroy the plant.

Physical controls: Adults will be unable to access vulnerable vegetable crops if covered with a floating row cover. Plant different flowering herbs in your garden to attract helpful insects that will help eradicate leafminers.

MEXICAN BEAN BEETLES

The Mexican bean beetle is one of the most prevalent pests in vegetable gardens.

Identification: Adult Mexican bean beetles are copper-colored ladybug-like bugs with sixteen black spots. Their larvae have delicate, bristly spines and are pale yellow.

Plants affected: These insects and their larvae may be found in many types of beans, including green, snap, pole, runner, lima, and soy.

Description of damage: Adults and larvae eat down to the veins of the leaves. They also eat flowers and beans on occasion. The larvae are frequently seen on the undersides of leaves.

Preventative measures: Plant lots of blooming companion herbs to attract predatory bees that feed on the beetle larvae.

Physical controls: Cover bean plants with floating row covers from germination to flowering.

SLUGS AND SNAILS

Slugs are one of the most disliked pests in vegetable gardens.

Identification: Slugs and snails are mollusks that live on land. Snails have a shell, but slugs do not. They come in various colors, including black, gray, orange, brown, tan, and speckled, and they frequently leave a slime trail behind.

Plants affected: Slugs and snails are troublesome pests and like to consume young seedlings, so no list of vegetable garden pests would be complete without them. Slugs and snails eat a wide range of plant and vegetable species.

Description of damage: Snails and slugs eat leaves, leaving uneven holes in the borders and centers. Because they eat at night or on wet days, they cannot be seen during the day.

Preventative measures: Slugs and snails enjoy moist foliage, so water only in the morning. Snakes, birds, frogs, and toads like to eat slugs and snails; hence these should be encouraged in the garden. Commercial barriers made of copper strips fastened around plants prevent slugs and snails from eating them due to the chemical interaction with their slime.

Physical controls: Slugs can be handpicked and placed in a container with soapy water. Beer traps are also effective. However, the beer must be drained and replaced regularly.

SQUASH BUGS

These mating squash bugs will soon begin laying bronze-colored eggs that will hatch into more leaf-sucking squash bugs.

Identification: No list of vegetable garden pests would be complete without mentioning squash bugs, arguably the most difficult vegetable pest to treat. Adult squash bugs have flattened oval-shaped bodies and are about 5/8 inches long. The larvae are grayish and have black wings. They frequently eat in groups. Squash bug eggs are bronze in color and are found in clusters.

Plants affected: All cucumber family members, including cucumbers, zucchini, squash, melons, and pumpkins, are susceptible to squash bugs.

Description of damage: Adults and nymphs use their needle-like mouthpart to suck plant fluids. Leaves that have been damaged are speckled with yellow and finally become yellow and perish. In the event of a heavy infestation, plants may become crispy.

Preventative measures: Rotate crops, and use trellises to keep vines off the ground as much as possible.

Physical controls: From the time you plant until flowering starts, use floating row covers. Remove egg clusters with a piece of tape daily; be careful to inspect the leaf undersides since that is where most egg-laying happens.

SQUASH VINE BORERS

Although adults of the squash vine borer are rarely observed, the female deposits eggs on the vines.

Identification: Adult squash vine borers are huge wasp-like red and black moths. The larvae of these caterpillars are plump white caterpillars that live inside the base of squash vines.

Plants affected: All squash, including summer and winter squash, pumpkins, melons, and gourds, are vulnerable. However, this disease seldom damages cucumbers.

Description of damage: Borers are known to cause the quick withering of plants. Confirmation can be found by looking for a hole in the stem tissue around ground level.

Preventative measures: As soon as the first true leaves show, wrap a piece of aluminum foil around the base of the plant to protect it from egg-laying females.

Physical controls: Plants should be covered with a floating row cover shortly after being planted; this should be left in place until blossoming begins. If a borer hole is discovered before the plant dies, cut the stem open, scoop out the borer, and fill the wound with earth.

TOMATO HORNWORMS

Like their tobacco hornworm counterparts, tomato hornworms are a problem in the vegetable garden.

Identification: Adult hornworms have brown or gray wings and are huge nocturnal moths. Hornworm caterpillars have a soft horn or spike projecting from their rear and white stripes on the side of their body.

Plants affected: Plants that are impacted include tomatoes, potatoes, peppers, eggplants, and tobacco, which are all members of the tomato family.

Description of damage: The feces of tomato and tobacco hornworms are left behind as black pellets. Eaten leaves, usually found at the tops of the plants, are the most common source of damage. During the day, the caterpillars feed and rest on the leaves.

Preventative measures: Plant a lot of blooming herbs with tiny blooms near sensitive plants. These flowers draw tiny parasitic cotesia insects that utilize hornworms as hosts for their young, killing the hornworm.

Physical controls: Inspect plants for hornworms regularly and hand-pick those with the white, rice-like nests of honey bees dangling from their backs.

WHITEFLIES

Whiteflies are pests that drain plant liquids and cause deformed development in vegetable gardens.

Identification: Whiteflies are moth-like flies that are small and white. Infested plants are generally covered with sticky honeydew, the flies' feces. Whiteflies can be seen in vast numbers on the undersides of leaves.

Plants affected: Sweet potatoes, tomatoes, peppers, citrus, and other typical whitefly hosts in the vegetable garden include tomatoes, sweet potatoes, peppers, and citrus, among others.

Description of damage: Both whitefly adults and nymphs suck plant fluids, resulting in weak plants, wilted, yellow leaves, and, in severe cases, dropped leaves.

Preventative measures: Before acquiring fresh plants from a nursery, thoroughly examine them for whiteflies.

Physical controls: To trap adult flies and prevent a future generation, hang yellow adhesive cards slightly over the plant tops.

WHAT ARE ORGANIC PESTICIDES?

When it comes to organic farming, a common misconception is that no chemicals are used, but this is simply not true. Pesticides are a vital element of the growing process for farmers and gardeners since they protect and sustain crops all year. The main difference between standard chemical pesticides and organic pesticides is that organic pesticides use naturally occurring chemicals rather than synthetic compounds.

Organic gardeners begin by enriching the soil with organic substances like well-rotted compost or homemade garden compost, and traditional fertilizers use bone meal or fish blood.

The Benefits of Natural Pesticides

There are several reasons you should choose to use natural insecticides and cultivate your crops more organically. First and foremost, it is better for the environment since going organic reduces pollution and eliminates introducing new poisons into your soil, plants, and, eventually, your food.

Many gardeners value their health, and there is rising concern about the exposure to chemicals used in gardening and farming. Going organic can help to decrease contact with these potentially dangerous substances. Organic gardening also allows you to have a more holistic experience with gardening.

Many fantastic items are available to assist even the most inexperienced gardeners in growing a rich and robust vegetable garden. However, the disadvantage is that they often miss the opportunity to connect deeply with the soil. Organic gardening and natural pesticides require a thorough knowledge of your soil, your garden's insects, and how each plant functions. This is not a burden for dedicated gardeners; instead, it is a significant advantage for many.

Another thing worth mentioning here is the practice of companion planting. Companion planting can help to deter pests by attracting beneficial insects like lacewings and ladybirds to feed on pests. Moreover, companion planting can produce strong scents that confuse pests and compels them to abandon the crops.

EIGHT NATURAL AND HOMEMADE INSECTICIDES

Nothing beats the feeling of producing what you eat and knowing that you created your own insecticides. However, it is essential to know that just because they are homemade or natural, it does not mean that they are harmless. Before using any homemade insecticide, do your research and choose an effective and safe approach for you and your garden. Below are some natural and homemade insecticides you can use for your garden:

1. Vegetable Oil Spray

A homemade pesticide produced from vegetable oil and a light soap can effectively protect against aphids, mites, thrips, and other pests.

To produce a basic vegetable oil spray insecticide, mix one cup of vegetable oil with one tablespoon of soap (cover and shake properly). When you are ready to use it, mix two teaspoons of the vegetable oil spray blend with one quart of water, shake carefully, and spray directly on the faces of the plants affected by the pests. Because the oil penetrates the insects' bodies, it effectively suffocates them by blocking the pores through which they breathe.

2. Soap Spray

A soap spray, which is quite similar to the oil spray, is likewise suitable for killing mites, aphids, beetles, and other hungry small insects.

Mix one and a half tablespoons of a moderate liquid soap with one liter of water and spray the mixture directly on the affected surfaces of the plants to produce a basic soap spray insecticide. A soap spray insecticide works in the same manner as an oil spray pesticide does, and it may be used as needed. When using this approach, it is best not to apply it during the sunny part of the day but rather in the evenings or early mornings.

3. Neem Oil Spray

A potent natural pesticide produced from the seeds of the neem tree, neem oil, can interrupt the life cycle of insects (adult, larvae, and eggs), making it a valuable resource for organic gardeners.

Neem oil serves as a hormone disruptor and an "antifeedant" for pests that feed on plant components such as leaves. In addition, Neem oil is biodegradable and safe for dogs, birds, and other wildlife and a natural fungicide that may fight powdery mildew and other fungal problems on plants. It is available at a variety of garden stores and natural food markets.

Follow the instructions on the pack to apply neem oil. Alternatively, mix one teaspoon of light water detergent well with two teaspoons of neem oil. Use it directly on your crops to prevent infestation.

4. Diatomaceous Earth

This natural product with an odd name is made from diatomaceous earth, a sedimentary rock formed by fossilized algae, and is a rich resource. (It is believed to make up twenty-six percent of the planet's crust by weight.) One of the many uses for diatomaceous earth is as a natural pesticide. This material works by removing lipids (a waxy component) from the insects' exoskeletons, which subsequently dehydrates them to death, rather than poisoning or suffocating them.

Diatomaceous earth is commonly available at garden stores but is frequently only available in large bags, so if you have a tiny yard, try dividing it with a neighbor. To use, just dust the ground around your plants or sprinkle it on the leaves to help eliminate snails, slugs, and other crawling insects. Diatomaceous earth must be applied after every rain because of its dry characteristics.

5. Garlic Spray

Garlic is recognized for its pungent odor, which is tasty to some but unpleasant to others, and it is this powerful scent that is used as a natural pesticide. It is unclear if garlic and chili spray are insecticides or, more likely, insect repellents. Still, in any case, these basic cooking components can be used to reduce, if not eliminate, pest infestations in the yard.

Take two entire garlic bulbs and mix them with a tiny quantity of water in a food processor or blender to produce a basic garlic spray. Allow the mixture to lie overnight before draining it into a quart jar and adding half a cup of vegetable oil (optional), a teaspoon of light liquid soap, and enough water to fill the jar. To apply this pesticide, combine one cup of the mix with one quart of water and spray over the affected plants liberally.

6. Chili Pepper Spray

Chili pepper spray, like garlic spray, is an efficient organic insect repellent that may be used on a wide range of pests. Fresh, spicy chilis or hot pepper powder may be used to make a chili spray.

Mix one tablespoon of pepper powder with one quart of water and a few drops of light liquid detergent to produce a basic chili spray. This combination can be applied to the leaves of susceptible plants at maximum intensity. Allow it to cool completely before straining out the chili material and adding a few drops of liquid soap. Spray as desired.

7. All-in-One Homemade Spray

This all-in-one homemade natural pesticide is reported to be a compilation of several unique recipes. To make, pour one garlic bulb and one small onion into a blender, add one teaspoon of chili powder and soak for one hour. Next, filter the solution and stir in one spoonful of liquid soap until well combined. To use this homemade pesticide, spray it thoroughly on both the top and lower surfaces of the leaves. Keep the rest of the liquid in the fridge for up to a week if necessary.

8. Tomato Leaf Spray

Tomato plants belong to the nightshade family, which means they contain alkaloids like tomatine, which may successfully control aphids and other insects. To prepare a natural pesticide, combine two cups of fresh tomato leaves (from the plant's bottom) with one quart of water and soak overnight. Using a spray bottle, drain off the plant material and spray it onto the plant leaves.

ALTERNATIVE METHODS OF PEST CONTROL

Companion Planting (Intercropping)

This is a method in which two or more crops are grown concurrently on the same plot of land. It is also known as "companion planting" and has been practiced successfully in Latin America and Africa for thousands of years. According to research, companion planting or intercropping delivers higher yields on less land than single-crop farming. In addition, these strategies maximize resources and organize spontaneous biological processes that do not occur in conventional monoculture.

Companion planting is an alternative to pest control that better uses existing resources and brings people and the environment closer together by employing mutually beneficial gardening techniques. This technique reduces waste, soil degradation, and insect and disease issues. And finally, there will be fewer reasons to apply harsh chemical controls, which have been found to harm wildlife habitats and our health and well-being.

Benefits of Companion Planting or Intercropping

- Increases soil fertility, structure, moisture, and soil microbes
- Better organic pest management, often through their natural enemies
- Fewer weeds and more ground covered for more extended periods
- Less land is needed, resulting in better efficiency of natural resources
- Different sizes and shapes of plant roots make use of all the soil
- An organic way to protect your crops against diseases
- Crops planted together yield more varied and nutrient-rich contents
- Plants growing near other plant species often have better immunity against bacteria

Main Crop and Second Crop Method

This type of intercropping is especially beneficial when your primary crop is nutrient-deficient. Instead of being cultivated for harvest, the second crop is planted to improve the conditions of the main crop by supplying nutrients to the soil. Wheat (first crop) and beans (second crop) are notable examples.

Cover Cropping

A cover crop is a type of off-season crop planted throughout the winter. While the ground is resting, this replenishes it with goodness and nutrients. In addition, it is an environmentally friendly approach to managing soil health, fertility, and erosion.

It includes water conservation, weed control, and pest and disease control issues. This growth strategy encourages natural biodiversity while also benefiting animals.

The Benefits of Cover Cropping

- Decreases the need for tillage, conserving valuable soil nutrients and microbes
- Many cover crops, such as green manures, add nutrients to the soil
- Digging in cover crops helps to rebuild the soil's organic matter and stop soil erosion
- The ground is covered for more extended periods, resulting in better soil water retention and lower evaporation levels
- Deep and fibrous root systems help to break up heavy soils
- Protects bare ground over the winter months and reduces surface weeds

Examples of Cover Crops

- Buckwheat aids in weed suppression, enriches the soil and attracts beneficial insects.
- Clover and vetch are commonly used legume cover crops grown for their nutrient-rich, organic properties.
- Grazing rye is one of the top cover crops with a high ability to hold onto soil nitrogen.

- Legumes of all types, especially winter field beans and peas, add nitrogen to the soil.
- Mustard is a fast-growing foliage crop that will boost soil's organic content when dug in.

Crop Rotation System

Every good gardener knows how to develop and implement a vegetable crop rotation scheme. It is usually done every three or four years, and it is an excellent method to keep your crops and soil healthy year after year.

The essential thing to remember is to avoid planting the same crop in the same location for two years in a row. Thus, hungry predators can roam across the soil, replenishing the earth's nutrients.

Strip Cropping

Strip cropping is how most recreational gardeners grow their favorite vegetables by alternating rows of different plants. This approach does not exactly combine two crops but offers the same environmental advantages, such as nutrient cycling and soil erosion reduction. A nutrient cycle describes how nutrients move from the physical environment into living organisms and back. It is similar to ecological recycling and is essential to all ecosystems.

Trap Crops

The disappointment of meticulously cultivating a crop only to have it destroyed or ruined by pests like slugs, aphids, or other bugs is not uncommon. In cases like this, the general advice is to spray crops very thoroughly with pesticides, but many of us choose to use nature's organic control for our food. Trap cropping is an excellent practice that organic farmers employ daily, but only a few gardeners understand its advantages.

A trap crop or a sacrifice crop is a plant you put in your garden to keep pests away from your main crops. In the same way that an African will prefer African foods over Asian foods, pests also like some crops better than others. Therefore, pests will be drawn to the trap crop and will typically leave your primary crops alone if you plant rows of it near your vegetables. You do not need to harvest anything from your trap crop; its sole purpose is to keep pests away from the plants you want to grow. Here are some factors to consider before planning trap cropping:

Different Pests Prefer Different Trap Crops

The pests you aim to catch will determine which trap crop to use. It is vital to choose the proper plants because if they are not sufficiently appealing to the insect, they will be useless. This is usually a question of trial and error and observation of the pests' preferences in your garden.

The Layout of the Trap Crop

Planting the trap crop along the perimeter of your growth region may be adequate for some insects. Others are harder to eliminate, and it may be vital to interplant them to divert them away from the major crops. Quantities vary depending on the pest you are attempting to ward off, but farmers often set aside twenty percent of their primary crop area for the trap crop.

Timing

The majority of bug infestations occur during a given period of the year. For example, I always have an aphid infestation in my garden in late May or early June. Therefore my trap crop should be fully established by the time the pests arrive.

Beneficial Insects

Trap crops are only one component of successful organic pest control. They must be balanced with enough companion planting flowers to lure beneficial insects such as lacewings and ladybugs that eat the pests.

Examples of Trap Crop

Below are some examples of trap crops:

- Aphids (blackfly, greenfly, and whitefly) are attracted to nasturtium stems and will frequently fully cover them. Ants will likely be seen 'farming' aphids for their exuding honeydew.
- Nettles also attract aphids, and because they do so early in the season, beneficial insects like ladybugs are typically attracted to them.
- Slugs are believed to find chervil particularly appealing.
- Slugs, thrips, and nematodes are all drawn to French Marigold.
- Radishes are supposed to attract flea beetle and root fly away from cabbages, but other brassicas may also be utilized as trap crops; it's recommended to try Chinese cabbage and collards.

Do They Work?

Yes, they do work. Trap crops are incredibly effective in my experience, but it is essential to recognize that they are only one part of the puzzle. A variety of plants reduces the likelihood of settling on the primary crop and should be included in any companion planting scheme.

COMMON PLANT DISEASES TO BE AWARE OF

Here are some of the most frequent diseases to watch out for when growing crops in your garden.

BACTERIAL LEAF SPOT

As the name suggests, bacterial leaf spot is caused by microscopic bacteria infiltrating your plant's foliage. It creates blotches on the leaves and discoloration in lesser cases. It can even kill the leaves in the most severe circumstances.

This disease thrives in cold or damp environments. If you water from above and the dirt splashes on the leaves, the bacteria in the soil might spread to the plant's leaves.

Germs can breed in any weeds or plants left in your garden if you don't clear them up over the winter. Then, the problem may resurface when you plant anything fresh in your garden the following year.

Solution

A few basic measures are required to prevent this condition. To begin with, avoid spraying dirt on your plants by watering them from beneath. It is also a good idea to water your plants early in the day. If bacteria from the ground splashes onto your plant, you will be providing an excellent breeding place for them.

Water your plants early in the day to allow them to dry up before the cool evening air arrives. If you water late in the day, you are supplying moisture and low temperatures, which encourage germs to spread. Ensure that you clean out your garden each year. Leave no weeds or dead plants in the growing area since this acts as a breeding ground for various pests and illnesses.

RUST

Rust is a good word for this condition since it accurately describes how it appears. It will cause discoloration in your plant's leaves, making it appear rust is developing on them. Rust is a fungus that spreads through the air in damp situations. The spores will fall on plant leaves and begin to reproduce. Eggplant, okra, onions, artichokes, asparagus, beans, sweet potatoes, peas, and maize are typically the most affected vegetables.

Solution

Prevention is the best approach to avoiding rust. This starts when you plant your crops. To minimize conges- tion, make sure you use suitable thin- ning procedures. Improve the air circulation around your crops by

spacing them optimally. Better ventilation reduces the amount of mois- ture trapped within the plant, making it a less desirable breeding ground for disease.

It is also a good idea to water plants from below or early in the day. This allows the plants to stay dry, so there is less risk of spreading disease.

Don't forget to keep your garden in good shape as well. At the end of each growing season, tidy up the garden area to decrease the possibility of pests hanging about throughout the winter. If your plants have been affected by rust, remove any damaged leaves from them. Also, apply an organic fungicide designated for rust treatment to the remainder of the plant. Then, to limit the odds of a future epidemic, follow the proce- dures outlined above.

DOWNY MILDEW

Downy mildew is a fungal infection as well. Downy mildew prefers wet, chilly environments, as do other fungal infections. It spreads through the air and water, showering dirt onto plants, your hands, and equip- ment. Discoloration of the leaves is the first sign of this illness. Downy mildew will gradually grow grey hairs that will infect your plant and damage the leaves as it spreads.

Solution

Downy mildew may be prevented by using soaker hoses to irrigate your plants from below. You may also water early in the day to allow the plants to dry up before the nighttime chill sets in. When working with plants that appear to be unhealthy, make sure to clean your hands and gardening tools. Any infected plants should be removed and killed to prevent future disease transmission.

An organic fungicide can be used to treat downy mildew if it is caught early. You can also choose to plant disease-resistant varieties of your preferred crops to increase your chances of completely avoiding this illness.

EARLY OR LATE BLIGHT

Blight affects many vegetables, although tomatoes and potatoes are the most affected. Early blight emerges as black blotches on the plant's soil level. Late blight shows as black patches on the stem that spread to the plant's leaves.

This virus may survive the winter in the soil and is most commonly transferred to plants when the dirt is sprayed onto the plant while watering.

Solution

Tidy up your garden at the end of every season to keep blight away from your crops. Pests and diseases love plant residues and weeds. Water your plants at the soil level using soaker hoses or water earlier in the day to give them enough time to dry before nighttime temperatures hit. If your plant has been infected with early or late blight, use an organic fungicide. To keep the condition under control, you may have to treat it more regularly. When a plant appears to be sick, rescue it, uproot it, and kill it to prevent the disease from spreading to other nearby plants.

CORN SMUT

Corn smut is an abnormal condition that can develop in your garden. Although this disease can wreak havoc on your corn yield, it is not seen as a downside in some communities. Instead, it is seen as a delicacy used as a stuffing in quesadillas. Although this fungus is edible, its striking appearance makes it difficult to overlook. Corn smut has the potential to reduce your corn crop. This disease creates massive growths above the ground on any section of the maize plant.

It is dispersed by wind and water and can spend the winter in the soil. It does, however, appear to thrive in dry, hot conditions. Corn smut can survive in the ground for up to seven years, making it difficult to eradicate. It infects plants by exploiting any previous damage. Corn smut sees an opportunity and seizes it.

Solution

Plant disease-resistant maize cultivars first to avoid corn smut. Then, try to keep your corn crop from being harmed. If you have a pest infestation, treat it with a pesticide as soon as you notice it to prevent the fungus from getting into the corn.

When fertilizing, be sure to use a well-balanced fertilizer, and if some of your crops have been infected with corn smut, uproot and destroy them right away to prevent the disease from spreading.

CLUBROOT

Clubroot infection grows in acidic soil. It is a fungus that primarily affects brassica plants. The most commonly affected crops are broccoli, turnips, cauliflower, Brussels sprouts, cabbage, and radishes. This infection is usually detected when the crop's growth slows down. After further study, pull up the plant and note the crop's thick roots. This is a dead giveaway of a clubroot infection.

Solution

Increasing the pH of your soil is the most effective way to prevent club-root infection. The pH level should be at least 7.0, although it can go up to 8.0. Putting lime in your vegetable garden might help raise the pH of your soil. Use a soil test kit to ensure that the soil is at the correct level.

If clubroot is present in your soil, it can live there for two decades. Therefore, if your plants have been infected with clubroot disease, you should uproot them completely. This involves removing every portion of their root system, as the infection will spread if you do not do so. When removing sick plants, always sanitize any gardening tools you use.

BLOSSOM END ROT

The disease primarily affects tomatoes and pepper plants, causing rotting bottoms. If you see it in your garden, do not worry, because if you manage to take care of your plants quickly, you can still get good crops. Blossom end rot is a symptom that your soil is deficient in calcium.

Solution

You can mitigate this issue by spraying powdered milk at the bottom of your plants as you are planting them. If you did not put powdered milk at the base of your plants before growing them, it is never too late to do so. Just sprinkle powdered milk around the base of your plants. It is affordable and should give enough calcium to boost your yield.

MOSAIC VIRUS

Mosaic virus is a disease you do not want to come across in your garden. The reason is that the symptoms differ depending on the plant, and there is not much you can do once it has developed. This is a virus that gardeners usually carry through their crops. Because many of us hardly wash our hands with soap when handling our garden plants, we accidentally touch a sick plant and spread it to another.

Curled leaves, stunted development, yellowing of leaves, and a diminished yield are all indications of this disease. However, some mosaic virus-infected plants show symptoms that mislead gardeners to believe they are suffering from an entirely different virus.

Solution

If you find the mosaic virus in your soil, the first thing you should do is uproot and kill any affected plants. Then, sanitize everything that came into touch with the contaminated plants. So, sanitize your clothes, hands, and all garden equipment. Unfortunately, there is no chemical treatment for this disease as of now.

VERTICILLIUM WILT

Verticillium wilt is a dreadful disease that can wreak havoc in your garden. One of the first symptoms is curled foliage, then browning and withering. Finally, your plant may die. This illness is caused by a fungus that enters your crop through the ground. It works its way through the plant's system, killing it in the end, and it most usually affects tomatoes, peppers, cucumbers, potatoes, and pumpkins.

Solution

There is nothing you can do if your plants have been affected by verticillium wilt except uproot and kill them. Your garden is still not safe after you have wiped out the fungus. So, you have two choices to mitigate this issue. The first choice is to cultivate disease-resistant vegetables. Another method is to use solarization to destroy the fungus in the soil.

You will need to dig up to six inches of soil in your garden area. Using a lawn hose, thoroughly wet the area before covering it with plastic. Keep the plastic sealed for a minimum of one month. Warm temperatures and sunshine are required throughout the month to sufficiently heat the soil to destroy the fungus that has taken up residence there. After that, your soil should be healthy.

DAMPING OFF

Damping-off is a fungus that mainly affects young seedlings. It happens when the seedlings' stems and roots decay.

Solutions

There is no correcting this sickness once it has infected your seedlings. Your best chance is to stay away from it entirely. To begin with, sanitize your soil. This will eliminate any hidden pathogens in the ground before you grow anything. Do the same thing with any containers or pans to start seedlings. You can sanitize by raising the soils temperature to 180 degrees F. (82 C.) for 30 minutes. You can do this via, oven, steaming, or microwave.

When planting seeds, keep in mind that the depth at which they are planted is important. You will overwork them during germination if you plant them too deeply. The plant will become stressed and prone to disease. Also, keep adequate spacing in mind. Airflow will be improved if there is enough space around the plant. This is the opposite of the disease's ideal breeding habitat.

Prevention of Disease

Growing healthy plants consistently is the easiest and most cost-effective strategy to prevent plant disease in your garden. Plants that have been damaged by drought, low fertility, or weed competition are more sensitive to disease-causing agents. If sickness is prevented before it develops, infected plants are hardly ever restored to strong, healthy, productive development. Plant disease may be avoided by following the simple measures below.

- Maintain vigorously growing, healthy plants
- Avoid over-watering or planting in poorly drained soils
- Use fertilizers and pesticides only as directed
- Use drip irrigation
- Do not cultivate or harvest when plants are wet
- Apply mulch
- Monitor crops
- Maintain a cleanliness program
- Choose resistant varieties

SEVEN HOMEMADE FUNGICIDES TO TRY

If you do not want to use harsh pesticides on the foods you produce, making your own fungicide treatments is a good solution. Fungicide treatments that are effective and safe may be manufactured at home and will save you a considerable amount of money. No special ingredients are required. In fact, you may even have everything you need in your kitchen right now.

Why Use Homemade Fungicides?

Saves Money

Fungicides from the store may be quite expensive, and many of them include chemicals that are harmful to your health and the environment. Harsh chemicals can also be found in certain organic sprays.

Fewer Chemicals

Most DIY fungicide sprays are safe to use on decorative plants, vegetables, herbs, and perennials, and they will safeguard your plants from that pesky fungus. Below are some homemade fungicides:

1. Powdery Mildew Fighter

Powdery mildew is a gardener's worst fear. It shows up on the foliage of your plants as a fine, ashy covering. Not only is it unattractive, but it also weakens and destroys plants over time. Powdery mildew is stopped in its tracks with this DIY fungicide. It can also be used to treat black spots on flowers.

Ingredients

- Four teaspoons of baking soda
- One teaspoon of mild soap
- One gallon of water

To make the spray, combine all components in a spray container and shake well. Spray all affected leaves from top to bottom, making sure the liquid is thick enough to drain off. Next, spray the whole plant, not just the affected leaves, because the fungus may be hidden.

2. Tomato Fungicide

Tomatoes are one of those plants that most of us enjoy growing, yet they are prone to fungi. Here is how to protect your tomato plants against fungus.

Ingredients

- One bulb of garlic
- Two tablespoons of canola oil
- Four hot peppers
- Juice from one lemon

Combine all of the ingredients in a bucket and steep overnight. Strain the mixture the next day to remove all particles using a sieve or cheesecloth. Fill a spray bottle halfway with water and add four teaspoons of this mixture. When a fungal illness is detected, spray both the top and bottom of the leaves.

3. Apple Cider Vinegar

To make a gallon of apple cider vinegar spray, combine four tablespoons of apple cider vinegar with a gallon of water. To avoid the acid and sunlight from burning the leaves, use this solution early in the day. This spray is effective against black spots, leaf spots, and mildew and may be used as a preventive spray every few weeks.

4. Horseradish

Mix one cup of horseradish and sixteen ounces of water. Allow to soak for at least twenty-four hours. In the morning, add two cups of water. This should be sprayed freely all over your plants.

5. Cornmeal

This is yet another easy-to-make fungicide. This spray has worked well on fruit trees, roses, and zucchini. Mix one cup of cornmeal and five gallons of water. Drain after twenty-four hours and apply straight to the leaves of the plant.

6. Aspirin

This miracle medication, which has been used to treat humans for millennia, is also a garden marvel. So far, so good. I have seen great results using this fungicide. You will need one aspirin and four cups of water. Crush the aspirin and add the aspirin powder to the water. During the growth season, spray your plants liberally every couple of weeks. As a prophylactic measure, spritz this combination every two weeks or so.

7. Painted Daisies

The dried leaves of the colored daisy are used to make pyrethrin. It is a simple plant to grow and has a strong antifungal effect. To make the powder, just dry a few handfuls of leaves and crush them. Soak in four gallons of water for twenty-four hours. Drain through linen and sprinkle on plants as a fungicide preventive and curative on any plant.

Using Your Homemade Fungicides

Spray a few leaves with your combination before covering the entire plant to determine whether it has any adverse effects. Some of the solutions are relatively strong, despite being natural. It is good to spray early in the season before any fungal concerns arise because it may be tough to deal with fungi after they develop.

Always use natural, safe substances, and do not be scared to try something new. Like other gardeners, I have lost a lot of plants to fungal diseases in the past. While you may never be able to eliminate fungi completely, you can reduce the damage and preserve as many plants as possible. You will need to experiment to see what works best for your particular plants.

To prevent infestation and check what is wrong with your plant, follow any of the following steps.

- Check plants regularly → Any noticeable changes? → Diagnosis of pest/diseases → Treatment method → Preventative measures for the future
- Add Fungicides →Plant your garden → Check plants regularly, →and add preventive measures for the future.

CONCLUSION

You have now learned about the common pests that you can see in your garden and how to control them. You have also learned about pesticides and fungicides and their preparation. We all agree that chemicals are hazardous to our plants, so we will use homemade pesticides and fungicides. I think that is great. But, do not forget to test your soil and plants before applying any preventive methods. Also, test these methods over a small area before using them on the entire garden.

6

WEED MANAGEMENT

I magine a situation where unwanted guests visit your house. They share your food and the little water you have, which is insufficient for your family's needs and even compete with you for bed space. That is how weeds work. They compete with your crops for space, water, nutrients, and every available resource.

My friend told me a story of when she left her vegetable garden in her husband's care. He was supposed to monitor the crops because she had just planted them a week before traveling. Although he was swamped at that time, he gave her his word that he would take care of the plants. Eventually, his work became more demanding, so he forgot about the crops. When he remembered, the weeds were already sprouting.

If he had let her know, she could have advised him on what to do. He decided to take care of the situation himself. Because he was a novice, the best he could do was weed by hand. Although he was able to pull out the weeds, it took him a lot of time and energy. When my friend came home her husband mentioned how hard it was to upkeep and weed a garden.

Yes, he successfully removed the weeds by hand; but he also promised not to do so again. I know that there would be no need for that type of weeding had my friend been home to guide him on what to do. This is because she knows effective weed control tricks, and I will share these tricks with you. I have used these tricks to stay on top of weed problems over the years, and they have always worked for me. The best part is that they will work for other people too. But first, let us learn about weeds.

WHAT ARE WEEDS?

Weeds are not a new thing and are present in all lawns and gardens. They are usually known as bad a thing. As I said earlier, weeds compete with your crops for light, water, space, and nutrients. Although some weeds are useful or beautiful, the majority are considered problematic. Knowing more about weeds can help you determine if these weeds should be tolerated or destroyed. Let us look at the types of weeds and how we control them.

Types of Weeds

Weeds are generally categorized as annual, biennial, or perennial.

Annual weeds: Annual weeds grow and spread via seed and have a one-year lifespan. They grow during summer and winter. Chickweed, for example, germinates in late summer or early fall, goes dormant throughout the winter, and blooms in the spring. Summer annuals like lamb's quarters sprout in the spring, grow during the summer, and then die when the winter season arrives.

Biennial weeds: Biennial weeds have a two-year lifespan. The first year sees them germinate and form rosettes, and in the second year, they blossom and produce seeds. Examples include garlic mustard and bull thistle.

Perennial weeds: Perennial weeds come back year after year, and in addition to seeds, they usually produce long taproots. These weeds are the hardest to eliminate. These include plantain, dandelions, and purple loosestrife.

COMMON WEEDS TO LOOK OUT FOR

DAISY – BELLIS PERENNIS

These are among the most common weeds and are hated by almost every gardener. They are evergreen perennials with rosettes of leaves growing on short, shallow-spreading rhizomes (underground stems). The rhizome continues to split into two, creating a daisy patch that increases in size year after year. This weed blooms throughout the year, though mainly from March to October, reaching a peak in April and May. At night and in wet conditions, the flower heads close up. Affected crops include lettuce, chicory, endive, etc.

NIPPLEWORT – LAPSANA COMMUNIS

Nipplewort is a common weed that emerges between June and September. The yellow blooms resemble other weeds of the same family, like smooth sowthistle and hawkweed. The leaves are gently hairy and occur alone rather than in pairs. Affected crops include salsify, Jerusalem artichoke, globe artichoke, etc.

RAGWORT – SENECIO JACOBAEA

Although one of the few plants listed under the Noxious Weeds Act, ragwort may be found in abundance across the countryside. As a result, it will undoubtedly make its way into gardens, and it will then settle itself on the lawns. It is commonly classified as a biennial plant. Still, it may flower after more than two years and can also be classified as a short-lived perennial. It is usually seen between June and November. Affected crops include salsify, Jerusalem artichoke, globe artichoke, etc.

DANDELION – TARAXACUM OFFICINALE

Almost everyone recognizes dandelions, with their bright yellow flowers and seed heads; they appear everywhere in late March and early

April when in full bloom. They are perennials with a distinctive taproot and rosette of leaves that recover quickly after being removed or hoed away. When fully ripe, the seeds resemble microscopic parachutes, allowing them to be blown and spread by the wind. Affected crops include salsify, Jerusalem artichoke, globe artichoke, etc.

HAIRY BITTER CRESS – CARDAMINE HIRSUTA

This weed grows in gardens and nurseries rather than in fields. Hairy Bitter Cress grows prolifically, and it can be introduced unintentionally by purchasing a container plant at a garden center. Its first leaves are kidney-shaped, and the cotyledons are oval. The mature leaves are rather distinctive, and this, along with the little white blooms, makes it a fairly simple weed to recognize. It is a versatile weed since it can blossom and set seeds as a little plant. When the seed capsule is ready, it can propel the seeds up to sixteen feet away, and you can feel the seeds striking your hand when weeding mature plants with your hands. Affects crops include cabbage, sprouts, broccoli, etc.

FIELD BINDWEED – CONVOLVULUS ARVENSIS

This weed is much smaller than the hedge bindweed; it is far less common and clings to the ground. The leaves are different from hedge bindweed. The lobes are sharp, and the tip is typically curved, especially as the leaf grows. It tends to survive due to its underground rhizomes. The flowers are pink in color, and they bloom during the summer.

PETTY SPURGE – EUPHORBIA PEPLUS

Petty spurge blooms are small, but the plant is unique and unlikely to be mistaken for anything else. Except for its larger sibling, the sun spurge, petty spurge is a much smaller plant in height and leaf size. This weed has some latex that can be used to treat some skin cancers and grows to about a foot high

ANNUAL MERCURY – MERCURIALIS ANNUA

This weed usually grows on waste ground, mainly on light soil. It is an annual weed with smooth leaves and grows at a slow rate. It blooms from July to October and has male and female flowers on different plants.

BLACK MEDICK – MEDICAGO LUPULINA

This is a common weed that grows on roadsides, waste areas, in grassland, and even on lawns. It grows well in drained calcareous soils and avoids acidic environments. Black Medic blooms from May to August, and the leaves are gently hairy and have a tiny point at the top of each leaflet which distinguishes it from yellow clover. Affected crops include beans and peas.

RED CLOVER – TEIFOLIUM PRATENSE

Red clover is less common in gardens than its white and yellow counterparts, but it is abundant in fields, pastures, and roadsides. It is commonly used as organic manure since it fixes nitrogen and generates a lot of dry matter. This weed grows from May through to September.

YELLOW CLOVER – TRIFOLIUM DUBIUM

This weed is also common in waste grounds, lawns, and pastures. It is easy to mistake it with other trefoils when there are just leaves and no flowers, but you will recognize it more easily from May to August when the flowers grow. The yellow flower heads have roughly ten to fifteen blooms per head, which sets them apart from T. micranthum, which only bears two to six flowers. Affected crops include beans and peas.

WHITE CLOVER – TRIFOLIUM REPENS

White clover is usually found in grassy areas. It is beneficial for gardens since it improves soil nitrogen and helps save money on fertilizer. It grows from May to September, and affected crops include beans and peas. Like yellow and red clover, it is a beneficial plant because it attracts bees that carry nectar from the flowers.

COMMON VETCH – VICIA CRACCA

Vetch comes in two varieties, both of which are very abundant. The common vetch is Vicia cracca, while the bush vetch is Vicia sepium. The bush vetch blooms from April through June. Vetch may become a problem in the garden if it roots itself in shrubs since its large roots and knotted branches make it difficult to remove. The flowers are often pea-shaped and range in color from the bush's drab purple to bright purple. Affected crops include peas and beans.

AMERICAN WILLOWHERB – EPILOBIUM CILIATUM

This weed grows up to twelve to forty inches. It has tiny (1/4 to 1/3 inch diameter) flowers, pale pink petals with deep clefts, and a club-shaped stigma. The lowest section of the stem is also reddish, which helps differen-tiate it. It is similar to broad-leaved Willowherb and hoary Willowherb, although the latter has slightly hairy leaves.

GREATER PLANTAIN – PLANTAGE MAJOR

Because it is tolerant of compact terrain, this robust ancient plant can be seen growing wild on disturbed ground, roads, tracks, and entrances. It can also be seen growing with its brother, ribwort plantain, on lawns.

CURLED DOCK – RUMEX CRISPUS

Curled docks are predominantly grassland weeds, although their capacity to colonize disturbed soils and waste areas may make them an issue in gardens. Unless curled dock infected grassland is dug up for a tillage crop, they are rarely a concern on arable land. Curled dock seeds may survive in the soil for decades, making them prolific seeders. Docks have a robust taproot system, making them difficult to eradicate. Any root left after digging out can grow again. Affected crops include rhubarb and so on.

SCARLET PIMPERNEL – ANAGALLIS ARVENSIS

The Scarlet Pimpernel is a common weed found in waste areas and vegetable gardens. It is easy to spot when it is in bloom thanks to its bright red blooms that open in the sun but close on cloudy or rainy days. It's easy to confuse it with chickweed when it's just a seedling, but keep these things in mind: The cotyledons are tiny, pointed, triangular plants growing near the ground. They are glossy, dark green, and triangular. The undersides of the first genuine leaves bear black markings, but the mature leaves are triangular, lustrous, and silky smooth. This harmless weed can be found in gardens, although it does not affect crop development.

SILVERWEED – POTENTILLA ANSERINA

This weed is common and abundant along roadsides, farm routes, waste ground, and field entrances. It is a creeping trailing plant growing from over-ground runners and can be a nuisance on verges.

SLENDER SPEEDWELL – VERONICA FILIFORMIS

Because it is resistant to most garden herbicides, this weed tends to persist once rooted in a garden. It may look lovely blooming in a long grass environment when in full blossom.

HELXINE – SOLEIROLIA SOLEROLII

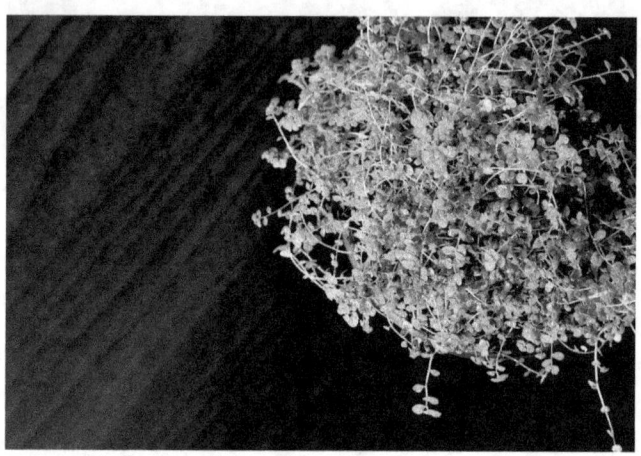

This stubborn weed is not very hardy since it gets blackened by cold, but it always recovers after a cold spell. This weed has an odd feature in that it never grows in the wild, preferring to stay near human settlements. It is a low-growing, mat-forming, evergreen perennial that grows in lawns, shrub borders, walls, and concrete slabs. It prefers the shadier areas of the garden as well. The leaves are small, and the stems are somewhat reddish.

COMMON NETTLE – URTICA DIOICA

Clusters of this weed can be seen growing in fields and around farm-yards. It is a sign of fertile soil and is especially common in phosphorus-rich environments. Common nettle is frequently found growing on top of old manure piles. It blooms from June to August.

WEED CONTROL OPTIONS

Since you know how harmful some weeds can be to your crops, you should know how to control them. Depending on the option that best suits you, it can be helpful to know these effective weed control options:

Mulching

Mulching is ideal for small spaces. However, it has the potential to slow or inhibit the growth of nearby plants. Some perennial weeds resist this control method, especially those whose food stores keep growing despite mulching. You can use grass cuts, hay, wood chips, etc., as mulch. Or use other coverings such as newspaper clippings to cover the soil. This may prevent sunlight from reaching the weeds; sunlight is necessary for weeds to survive.

Weed Fabric Barrier

Weed fabric barriers are often employed in mulched environments. They are usually installed when planting and mulching. However, fabric barriers and similar geotextiles are much more time-consuming and expensive to make than organic mulch barriers, especially when replacing the old fabric.

Solarization

Solarization is a method of raising the soil's temperature to the point where the weeds are killed. Soil solarization aids in releasing nutrients contained in the earth and eliminating unwanted weeds without pesticides. Soil solarization is accomplished by covering the soil with black plastic to collect solar rays. However, this impacts the soil's biological, physical, and chemical components, which may inhibit the development of other plants. This procedure will effectively halt photosynthesis and destroy weeds.

Roller Crimping

Roller crimping uses cover crops to help retain and improve the soil while also acting as a natural weed barrier. Roll crimping kills a cover crop by crushing the stems with the roller crimper's weight and blades. This stops seeds from growing or germinating further. While this environmentally friendly practice is best suited for small commercial vegetable farms, a home gardener may still do it on a modest scale.

While farmers may use commercial roller crimpers, home gardeners can use a leased sod roller or another heavy barrel pushed behind a lawnmower or ATV to produce a similar effect on a smaller scale.

Strip Tilling

This method is typically used in areas where soils have previously been substantially disturbed. Tilling is best done when the ground is still dry and before weed seeds have a chance to germinate. To till, turn the dirt over and cut the roots of the weeds at a depth of six inches to two feet. Then, to keep weeds at bay, till the upper six inches of the soil.

Mechanical

This process uses physical action or farm equipment to control the weeds. The weed type will determine the type of mechanical control to apply.

TEN WAYS TO PREVENT WEEDS

Never let them seed: Weeding should be done when the weeds are still young. Some weeds may generate thousands of seeds from a single plant, compounding your weed management issues for years. Make it a habit to check your garden every day. When they are young, pull weeds out or clip them off below the soil level. Keep your digging shallow to avoid bringing fresh weed seeds to the surface. Weeds are easy to eradicate when the ground is wet, such as the day after a new rain.

Clean gardening tools between areas: To avoid spreading weed seeds, clean your gardening tools as you move from one garden area to another. Removed weeds should not be left on the ground; instead, they should be discarded in the garbage.

Mow lawn regularly: To prevent lawn weeds from developing seed, mow your grass regularly.

Be careful when buying materials from garden centers: Request weed-free mulch, manure, compost, and soil. Also, check the label of your grass seed to be sure it does not include any other crop seed.

Cover a weedy patch with landscape fabric if you have time: Cover a weedy spot with landscaping fabric, black plastic, or an old carpet. Do this in the autumn, winter, or early spring, when your garden is not active.

Once you have seeded, do not till a garden area if it is filled with perennial weeds: If, after sowing, you realize that the area used in planting is filled with perennial weeds, never try to till it. Tilling is simply turning over and breaking up the soil. You will spread weeds to other parts of the garden.

Apply mulch: Mulch makes it difficult for weed seeds to germinate and inhibits sunlight. So, mulch it!

Water right around the plants: If you water your entire garden, you will merely be watering your weeds. So, eyes on your crop, gardener!

Do not under- or over-fertilize: This is straightforward. Under- or over-fertilizing your crops will encourage weed growth.

Establish a perimeter: Establish a weed-free perimeter around your potted plants, garden, or lawn by paying extra care to the area immediately next to the planted area. Lawns and plants should be mowed and mulched as they emerge, and weeds should be pulled or dug up. This will help reduce fresh weed seeds in the area you want to safeguard.

TAKEAWAY

If you have read this chapter, you have been given the knowledge to identify weeds in your garden and even know how to control them. The key takeaway from this chapter is that you do not want weeds lurking around in your garden. You have to inspect your garden regularly to detect any traces of weeds.

In the same way that early cancer detection can result in successful treatment, early detection of weeds can also result in a weed-free garden. Now that you know how to manage your garden effectively, let us discuss the possible pairings of crops you may want to grow in your garden. Learn how to work your garden correctly. The knowledge you will gain in the next chapter will complement what you have learned in this chapter.

7

GUIDELINES FOR THE BEST PAIRINGS AND PLANTING

S o far, you have learned the different types of gardening methods and how to control weeds and pests. You have also learned how to water your crops and where to situate them for the best sunlight.

Imagine a soccer match where the team manager decides to pair a striker and a defender in defense. Although both players will play, their pairing will not be as effective as pairing two defenders in defense. In the same way as a team manager is expected to pair the right players, a gardener is expected to pair the right crops.

I remember when one of my neighbors decided to grow a garden. The husband wanted to grow cabbages, while the wife wished for strawberries. They didn't have a big area to plant, so they agreed to grow both crops next to each other. I guess that is a sign of love. But guess what? Gardens don't see it that way. The outcome was not as good as they had hoped. Since then, they have decided to set aside emotions and pair the crops using the companion planting method.

Now, let us look at the best plant pairings that effectively complement each other and those that do not. Apart from learning the top best plant combinations for each plant, you will also discover how to grow them. If you are still with me, let's take a deeper dive!

COMPANION PLANTING FRIENDS AND FOES

ASPARAGUS

Top Companions That Benefit Asparagus

- **Basil** attracts pollinators and deters asparagus beetles.
- **Coriander** and **Dill** repel aphids.

Plants That Are Not Friendly With Asparagus

- **Potatoes** compete for nutrients in deep sections of the garden.
- **Onions** and **Garlic** will stunt the growth of asparagus.

Overview

Plant type: Vegetable

Soil pH: Neutral to Slightly Alkaline

Bloom time: Spring

Maturity time: Two to three years

When to plant: Early spring

How to plant: Plant crowns deep in the ground to shield them from yearly weed control cultivation. Dig up a hole of about 12 to 18 inches wide and 6 to 8 inches deep. Before planting, give the crowns a quick soak in lukewarm water.

How to harvest: Harvesting should be avoided throughout the first two seasons. Cut spears at ground level with scissors or a sharp knife.

Recommended varieties: Mary Washington, Apollo, Jersey knight,Guelph Millennium

BASIL

Top Companions That Benefit Basil

- **Peppers** provide excellent ground cover.
- **Marigolds** help repel many insects.
- **Borage** improves the health and flavor of basil.

Plants That Are Not Friendly With Basil

- When **Common Rue** and basil are planted together, both plants are stunted.
- **Thyme** thrives in a moist environment, whereas basil prefers a dry one.

Overview

Plant type: Herb

Soil pH: Slightly Acidic to Neutral

Bloom time: Summer

When to plant: Six weeks before last spring frost

How to plant: Sow seeds no more than 1/4 inch deep. For larger varieties, plant farther apart (about 16 to 24 inches).

How to harvest: Harvest in the early morning, when leaves are at their juiciest. Start harvesting basil leaves when plants are 6 to 8 inches tall.

Recommended varieties: Cinnamon basil, Purple basil, Thai basil

BEANS

Top Companions That Benefit Beans

- The roots of **Corn** and **Beans** occupy different layers in the soil. They do not compete for nutrients. Corn provides great support for the beanstalks to grow. This can free up some valuable space in the garden.
- **Potatoes** help repel Mexican bean beetles.
- **Rosemary** repels bean beetles.

Plants That Are Not Friendly With Beans

- **Onions** and **Garlic** plants discharge an antibacterial that kills the bacteria on the roots of the beans. This affects the bean's ability to fix nitrogen in the soil.

Overview

Plant type: Vegetable

Soil pH: Slightly Acidic to Neutral

Bloom time: Summer

Maturity time: Fifty to fifty-five days

When to plant: Sow immediately after the soil warms up to at least 48°F (9°C) following the last spring frost date. Planting too early can delay germination and cause the seeds to decay due to the cold, damp soil.

How to plant: Bush beans should be sown in rows 18 inches apart, 1 inch deep, and 2 inches apart. Pole beans should be sown 1 inch deep and placed around supports.

How to harvest: The best time to harvest beans is early in the morning, when the sugar content is at its maximum. It is important to harvest green beans every day; the more you harvest, the more the beans will continue to grow.

Recommended varieties: French green beans, Snap beans, Italian/Romano

BEETS

Top Companions That Benefit Beets

- **Bush Beans** help promote nitrogen in the soil. This enriches the beets.
- **Lettuce** takes up open space near beets. As a result, its shallow roots do not compete for the beet's water.
- **Onion** repels sugar beet flea beetles and deters rabbits and deer.
- **Radishes** help loosen the soil, so the beets can grow strong.

Plants That Are Not Friendly With Beets

- **Pole Beans** will stunt the growth of the beets.
- **Chard** and beets attract the same pests. This can cause an infestation.

Overview

Plant type: Vegetable

Soil pH: Slightly Acidic to Neutral

Bloom time: Early spring

Maturity time: Two months

When to plant: Four to six weeks before first fall frost

How to plant: Seeds should be sown 12 inches deep and 1 to 2 inches apart in rows approximately 1 foot apart. Cover the seeds with a thin layer of soil after they have been sown.

How to harvest: Loosen the dirt surrounding the beet and lift it carefully out of the ground.

Recommended varieties: Chioggia, Formanova, Detroit Dark Red

BORAGE

Top Companions That Borage Benefits

- Borage repels one of **Tomato's** most common pest, the tomato hornworm.
- Borage keeps a common **Cabbage** pest at bay, the cabbage worm.
- Borage repels many insects that hurt **Strawberries**. It also attracts many helpful pollinators.

Overview

Plant type: Herb

Soil pH: Slightly Acidic to Neutral

Bloom time: Autumn

Maturity time: One year

When to plant: Early summer

How to plant: Sow seeds directly into the ground about 1/2 inch deep in clusters of 3 or 4 seeds and cover them with nutrient-rich soil or compost.

How to harvest: Use gloves when cutting leaves even in the kitchen. When snipping borage leaves, choose the younger ones since they will have fewer tiny hairs.

BROCCOLI

Top Companions That Benefit Broccoli

- **Chamomile** improves the flavor of broccoli.
- **Potatoes** and broccoli have different nutritional needs and will not compete with each other for resources.
- **Rosemary** helps drive pests away from the broccoli.

Plants That Are Not Friendly With Broccoli

- **Beans** fix nitrogen in the soil. This can be too much for the broccoli to tolerate.
- **Asparagus, Corn,** and **Pumpkins** are heavy feeders and compete for the same nutrients as broccoli.

Overview

Plant type: Vegetable

Soil pH: Slightly Acidic to Neutral

Bloom time: Spring or fall

When to plant: Early to mid-spring (depending on your climate) for an early summer crop, or in mid-to-late summer for a fall crop.

How to plant: Sow seeds 1/2 inch deep and 3 inches apart if starting seeds outdoors. When they reach a height of two to three inches, thin seedlings, spacing them 12 to 20 inches apart.

How to harvest: Harvest broccoli in the morning, just before the heads blossom, when the head buds are strong and tight. Remove the plant's heads, leaving at least six inches of stalk.

Recommended varieties: Green Goliath, Green Duke, Green Magic, Flash

BRUSSELS SPROUTS

Top Companions That Benefit Brussels Sprouts

- **Beets** help boost magnesium, which Brussels sprouts need.
- **Chamomile** helps enhance the flavor of Brussels sprouts.
- **Garlic** helps repel aphids and blight.

Plants That Are Not Friendly With Brussels Sprouts

- **Strawberries** inhibit the growth of Brussels sprouts.

Overview

Plant type: Vegetable

Soil pH: Slightly Acidic to Neutral

Bloom time: Summer

When to plant: Fall or early winter

How to plant: Sow seeds 12 inches deep. Sow seeds two to three inches apart if direct planting outdoors.

How to harvest: Sprouts develop from the stalk's base upwards. When sprouts reach approximately one inch in diameter, harvest them from the bottom.

Recommended varieties: Diablo, Falstaff, Jade Cross

CABBAGE

Top Companions That Benefit Cabbage

- **Borage, Sage,** and **Rosemary** deter the cabbage moth caterpillar.
- **Chamomile** enhances the flavor of cabbage with calcium, sulfur, and potassium.
- **Onions** keep away cabbage worms, cabbage loopers, and aphids.
- **Pole Beans** provide partial shade.

Plants That Are Not Friendly With Cabbage

- **Rue** and cabbage should not be planted together.

Overview

Plant type: Vegetable'

Soil pH: Neutral

Bloom time: Spring and fall

Maturity time: Seventy days

When to plant: Sow seeds ¼ inch deep six to eight weeks before the last spring frost if beginning them indoors.

How to plant: Space seedlings 12 to 24 inches apart in rows, depending on the size of the desired head. The cabbage heads will get smaller the closer you put them.

How to harvest: Cut each cabbage head at its base with a sharp knife.

Recommended varieties: Primo, Cheers, Golden Acre, Gonzales

CARROTS

Top Companions That Benefit Carrots

- **Chives** improve the taste of carrots. Moreover, they have shallow roots that don't encroach on the carrots' space. They also deter carrot flies.
- **Legumes** help change nitrogen in the soil to the benefit of the carrots.
- **Nasturtiums** are a great trap crop to have in your garden. They lure pests, like aphids, away from your vegetables.

Plants That Are Not Friendly With Carrots

- **Parsnips** will attract the same pests making them more susceptible to the same diseases.
- **Potatoes** and carrots compete for space and will compete for soil nutrients.

Overview

Plant type: Vegetable

Soil pH: Neutral

Bloom time: Spring

Maturity time: Two months

When to plant: Two to three weeks before the last spring frost date.

How to plant: Sow 1/4 inch deep, 2 to 3 inches apart in rows 1 foot apart.

How to harvest: Hold them tightly at the base of the leaves, press down on the root, and slowly pull them upwards while twisting them.

Recommended varieties: Bolero, Danvers, Solar Yellow

CHERVIL

Top Companions That Benefit Chervil

- **Cilantro, Coriander,** and **Dill** grow well and thrive together.
- **Chervil** does best in part shade, as does lettuce. The lettuce can help shade some of the chervil.

Overview

Plant type: Herbs

Soil pH: Slightly acidic to neutral

Bloom time: Winter

Maturity time: Two years

When to plant: Two to three weeks before the last frost.

How to plant: Sow seeds in the ground when the soil temperature is between 55 and 65 degrees Fahrenheit, and you have two frost-free months ahead of you.

How to harvest: Chervil leaves are most delicious when they are young. Cut a whole branch from the base as needed; try to harvest the leaves while they are still small.

Recommended varieties: Crispum, Verissimo

CHIVES

Top Companions That Chives Benefits

- **Chives** are low maintenance. It is a beneficial herb that repels a lot of harmful garden pests. Only a handful of plants should not be planted with chives.

Plants That Are Not Friendly With Chives

- **Sage, Thyme, Rosemary**, and **Oregano** love dry, sandy soil, which is the opposite of what chives enjoy.
- **Beets** will stunt the growth of chives.
- **Pole Beans** seem to hinder the growth of chives.

Overview

Plant type: Herb

Soil pH: Slightly Acidic to Neutral

Bloom time: Summer

Maturity time: More than two years

When to plant: Spring and fall

How to plant: Sow seeds no more than 14 inches deep and 2 inches apart. Apply a thin layer of soil on top.

How to harvest: Cut the leaves down to the base when harvesting (within one to two inches of the soil).

Recommended varieties: Garlic chives

CILANTRO

Top Companions That Benefit Cilantro

- **Chervil** helps keep aphids at bay
- **Peas** are a great early-season plant that helps prepare the soil for many herbs.

Plants That Are Not Friendly With Cilantro

- **Fennel** is not a good companion to most herbs. **Cilantro** is no different. The substance secreted by fennel can inhibit growth.

Overview

Plant type: Herb

Soil pH: Neutral

Bloom time: Spring and fall

Maturity time: Six weeks

When to plant: After the danger of frost in the spring.

How to plant: Plant the seeds 1 to 2 inches apart in light, well-drained soil.

How to harvest: Harvest while the crop is low. Cut off the cilantro plant once the seeds have dropped and allowed it to self-seed.

Recommended varieties: Costa Rica, Long-standing

CORN

Top Companions That Benefit Corn

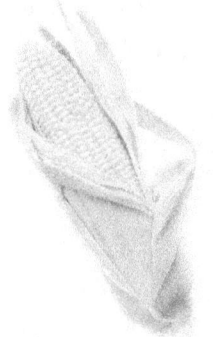

- **Pole Beans** provide much-needed nitrogen in the soil.
- **Cucumbers** create a ground cover for the corn. This helps control weeds and keeps the ground moist. **Melons** are similar.
- **Thyme** repels corn earworms.

Plants That Are Not Friendly With Corn

- **Cabbage** family plants are heavy eaters and will compete for food with corn.
- **Tomatoes** attract tomato hornworms. Planting them together will cause the tomato hornworm to come in greater numbers.
- **Fennel** is an herb you don't want around your vegetables. It can inhibit their growth significantly.

Overview

Plant type: Vegetable

Soil pH: Slightly Acidic to Neutral

Bloom time: Summer

When to plant: Two weeks after the last spring frost date.

How to plant: Moisten the seeds, cover them in damp paper towels, and keep them in a plastic bag for twenty-four hours to speed up the germination process. Space the rows 30 to 36 inches apart, and plant the seeds one to two inches deep and four to six inches apart.

How to harvest: To remove the stalk, pull the ears downward and twist.

Recommended varieties: Shrunken, Sugar-enhanced, Synergistic

CUCUMBERS

Top Companions That Benefit Cucumbers

- **Beans** boost nitrogen in the soil, which helps cucumbers grow.
- **Dill** attracts parasitic wasps that help pollinate your cucumbers and keeps pest levels down.
- **Marigolds** keep aphids away.

Plants That Are Not Friendly With Cucumbers

- **Melons** attract the same pests as cucumbers, making them more susceptible to those pests.
- **Potatoes** and cucumbers fight for the same food.

Overview

Plant type: Vegetable

Soil pH: Slightly Acidic to Neutral

Bloom time: Summer

When to plant: Two weeks after the last frost date.

How to plant: Plant seeds 1 inch deep and about 3 to 5 feet apart in a row.

How to harvest: Cut the stem above the fruit using a knife or clippers. The vine may be ruined if the fruit is pulled off.

Recommended varieties: Boston Pickling, Bush Crop, Lemon, Calypso

DILL

Top Companions That Dill Benefits

- Dill repels cabbage worms, spider mites, and cabbage loopers in **Cabbage, Collard,** and **Broccoli.**

Plants That Are Not Friendly With Dill

- Dill and **Carrots** are in the same family and can cross-pollinate.

Overview

Plant type: Herb

Soil pH: Slightly Acidic to Neutral

Bloom time: Summer

When to plant: Mid-summer

How to plant: Dill seeds should be planted approximately 1/4 inch deep and 18 inches apart.

How to harvest: Pinch off the leaves or cut them off with scissors.

Recommended varieties: Fernleaf, Bouquet, Mammoth

EGGPLANT

Top Companions That Benefit Eggplant

- **Beans** help boost nitrogen in the soil, which allows eggplants to grow.
- The strong scent of **Marigolds** deters many pests.
- **Spinach** helps retain moisture.

Plants That Are Not Friendly With Eggplants

- **Dill** and **Fennel** inhibit the growth of eggplants.

Overview

Plant type: Vegetable

Soil pH: Slightly Acidic to Neutral

Bloom time: Summer

Maturity time: Late summer (120 days)

When to plant: Six to eight weeks before the last spring frost date.

How to plant: Plant seedlings 24 to 30 inches apart in rows three feet apart.

How to harvest: The fruit will not come off if you pull it. Instead, use a sharp knife to cut the fruit. Gloves are recommended since the calyx can be thorny.

Recommended varieties: Black Bell, Black Beauty, Dusky

GARLIC

Top Companions That Benefit Garlic

- **Beets** take nutrients from different parts of the soil.
- **Carrots** deter some of the common pests that are attracted to garlic.
- **Spinach** helps control weeds since it grows low to the ground.

Plants That Are Not Friendly With Garlic

- **Sage** stunts the growth of garlic bulbs.
- **Parsley** competes for the same resources.

Overview

Plant type: Vegetable

Soil pH: Slightly Acidic to Neutral

Maturity time: Nine months

When to plant: Fall

How to plant: Plant cloves in an upright position, 4 to 8 inches apart and 2 inches deep. The wider root side should face down, and the pointed end should face up.

How to harvest: Carefully remove the bulbs using a garden fork. Yanking or pulling the stems by hand is not recommended.

Recommended varieties: Hardneck, Softneck, Great-headed

KALE

Top Companions That Benefit Kale

- **Beans** convert nitrogen in the soil.
- **Dill** attracts pollinators that increase the growth of kale.
- **Garlic, Chives,** and **Onions** help keep cabbage loopers, flea beetles, and aphids at bay.
- **Radishes** are a quick and easy harvest that does not crowd the kale. If you are limited on space, this is a great duo.

Plants That Are Not Friendly With Kale

- If members of the **Brassica** family are planted too close together, a pest infestation may occur as they attract the same pests.

Overview

Plant type: Vegetable

Soil pH: Neutral to Slightly Alkaline

When to plant: Four to six weeks before the last frost.

How to plant: Plant seeds 1/4 to ½ inch deep, 1 inch apart, in rows 18 to 30 inches apart.

How to harvest: Harvest a handful of leaves at a time, but not more than a third of the vine at a time.

Recommended varieties: Winterbor, Red Russian, Lacinato

LEEK (EARLY SEASON)

Top Companions That Benefit Leek

- **Celery** loosens the soil.
- **Carrots** deter leek moths and enhance the flavor of leek.
- **Melons** help keep the soil moist and act as a ground cover, preventing weed growth.

Plants That Are Not Friendly With Leek

- **Cabbage** and **Cauliflower** compete for the same nutrients.
- **Peas** and **Beans** attract harmful pests to the leek

Overview

Plant type: Vegetable

Soil pH: Slightly Acidic to Neutral

Maturity time: 75 days

When to plant: Spring

How to plant: Cover seeds with a light dusting of soil after scattering them on top of a healthy potting mix.

How to harvest: Simply twist and pluck them carefully. If the soil is dry, dig around them and pick them up.

Recommended varieties: King Richard, Lincoln

LETTUCE

Top Companions That Benefit Lettuce

- **Chervil** keeps slugs at bay.
- **Chives** and **Turnips** repel aphids.
- **Cucumbers, Corn,** and **Tomatoes** provide excellent shade.
- **Eggplants** improve the soil.

Plants That Are Not Friendly With Lettuce

- **Broccoli, Brussels Sprouts,** and **Cabbage** prevent seed germination.
- **Kale** and **Cauliflower** compete for nutrients.

Overview

Plant type: Vegetable

Soil pH: Slightly Acidic to Neutral

Bloom time: Spring and fall

When to plant: Two to four weeks before spring's last frost.

How to plant: Plant seeds 1/8 to 1/4 inch deep

How to harvest: Gently remove the outer leaves so that the center leaves can continue growing.

Recommended varieties: Red Leaf, Crisphead, Loose-leaf

MELON & WATERMELON

Top Companions That Benefit Melons

- **Beans** and **Peas** release nitrogen in the soil.
- **Lettuce** and **Spinach** keep the soil moist by providing ground cover.
- **Garlic** and **Carrots** loosen the soil.
- **Lavender, Oregano,** and **Chives** keep pests at bay.

Plants That Are Not Friendly With Melons

- **Squash** and **Zucchini** will compete for similar nutrients.
- **Corn** provides too much shade.

Overview

Plant type: Fruit

Soil pH: Slightly Acidic to Neutral

Maturity time: Around 90 days

When to plant: Four to six weeks before the date of your last spring frost.

How to plant: Plant seeds 1 inch deep, 18 inches apart

How to harvest: Pick fruit carefully by separating the stem from the fruit

Recommended varieties: Ambrosia, Athena, Bush Star

MINT

Top Companions That Mint Benefits

- Mint repels a **Carrot** pest called carrot flies.
- Mint helps **Cabbage, Cauliflower,** and **Kale** by deterring white cabbage moths and flea beetles.
- Mint is beneficial to **Eggplants** and **Tomatoes** since it repels aphids and mites.

Overview

Plant type: Herb

Soil pH: Neutral to Slightly Alkaline

Maturity time: Over two years

How to plant: Plant one or two plants in damp soil approximately 2 feet apart.

How to harvest: Cut the stems one inch from the ground

Recommended varieties: Corsican, Pennyroyal, Spearmint

MUSTARD GREENS

Top Companions That Benefit Mustard Greens

- **Chamomile** repels whiteflies.
- **Dill** attracts beneficial insects that reduce aphids and cabbage worms.
- **Garlic** may help deter rabbits with its smell.
- **Onions** help repel common pests that like mustard greens.

Plants That Are Not Friendly With Mustard Greens

- **Nightshades** are prone to verticillium wilt. This disease can wipe out your entire mustard greens crop.
- **Strawberries** attract slugs.

Overview

Plant type: Vegetable

Soil pH: Neutral

Bloom time: Warmer weather

Maturity time: Eighty to Ninety-five days

When to plant: Three weeks before your last frost date.

How to plant: Plant seeds 1 inch deep, 6 inches apart.

How to harvest: Remove seeds from the pods.

ONIONS

Top Companions That Benefit Onions

- **Lettuce** and **Spinach** keep the soil moist by providing ground cover.
- **Oregano, Parsley,** and **Dill** keep pests away.
- **Strawberries** and **Tomatoes** improve soil condition.

Plants That Are Not Friendly With Onions

- **Asparagus** takes away nutrients that onions need.
- **Beans** and **Peas** inhibit the growth of onions.
- **Leek** and **Garlic** attract pests.

Overview

Plant type: Vegetable

Soil pH: Neutral

Maturity time: About five months depending on the type

When to plant: Eight weeks inside before spring's last frost. Then transplanted outside in your garden just before the last frost.

How to plant: Plant seeds ¼ inch deep.

How to harvest: Carefully pull or dig onions up. Leave the top intact.

Recommended varieties: Buffalo, Copra, Stuttgarter, Candy

PEAS

Top Companions That Benefit Peas

- **Beans** add nutrients to the soil.
- **Carrots, Turnips,** and **Potatoes** help keep the soil loose.
- **Lettuce** and **Spinach** keep the soil moist by providing ground cover.
- **Peppers** repel aphids and spider mites.

Plants That Are Not Friendly With Peas

- **Garlic** and **Shallots** compete for similar nutrients.
- **Scallion** gives off harmful elements that can hurt the peas.

Overview

Plant type: Vegetable

Soil pH: Slightly Acidic to Neutral

Bloom time: Spring, fall

Maturity time: Sixty to seventy days

When to plant: Four to six weeks before the last spring frost date, six to eight weeks before your first fall frost date.

How to plant: Soak seeds in water overnight. Plant seeds 1 inch deep and 2 inches apart. Rows should be 7 inches apart.

How to harvest: Harvest peas once the dew has dried in the morning. Hold the vine with one hand and pull the pods off.

Recommended varieties: Lincoln, Little Marvel

PEPPERS

Companions That Help Peppers

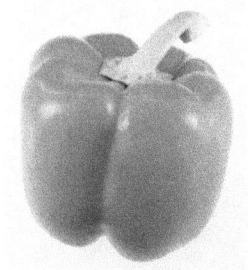

- **Asparagus** and **Chard** improve soil conditions.
- **Basil** helps trap heat and moisture.
- **Marjoram, Oregano**, and **Rosemary** deter common pests.
- **Tomatoes** help attract pollinators.

Plants That Are Not Friendly With Peppers

- **Beans** and **Peas** feed on similar nutrients.
- **Fennel** slows down growth.

Overview

Plant type: Vegetable

Soil pH: Slightly Acidic to Neutral

Bloom time: Summer

Maturity time: Sixty to ninety days

When to plant: Eight to ten weeks before your last spring frost date.

How to harvest: Use a sharp knife or scissors to cut peppers clean off the plant.

Recommended varieties: Lady Bell, Gypsy, Lipstick

POTATOES

Top Companions That Benefit Potatoes

- **Beans** deter Colorado potato beetles.
- **Chives** and **Onions** keep pests at bay.
- **Garlic** helps control potato blight.
- **Radishes** help loosen the soil.
- **Thyme** improves growth.

Plants That Are Not Friendly With Potatoes

- **Melons** and **Pumpkin**s take away nutrients from potatoes.
- **Peas** and **Beans** inhibit the growth of potatoes.
- **Berries** attract pests.

Overview

Plant type: Vegetable

Soil pH: Acidic

Maturity time: Eighty to a hundred days

When to plant: Two weeks after your last spring frost.

How to plant: Place the seed potatoes on the ground. Sprinkle with a soil-compost mixture. Cover them with sand or leaves and hill them up as the potatoes develop.

How to harvest: Gently dig potatoes up, taking care not to bruise the tubers.

Recommended varieties: Norland, Mountain Rose, Elba, Viking

RADISHES

Top Companions That Benefit Radishes

- **Brassicas** improve soil conditions.
- **Chervil** makes radishes hotter and crispier while keeping aphids at bay.
- **Dill** attracts beneficial insects.
- **Onions** and **Peppers** keep pests away.

Plants That Are Not Friendly With Radishes

- **Melons, Pumpkin**, and **Corn** take the needed sun away from the radishes.
- **Turnips** inhibit growth.

Overview

Plant type: Vegetable

Soil pH: Neutral

Bloom time: Summer

Maturity time: Three weeks

When to plant: Four to six weeks before the first fall frost.

How to plant: Sow seeds directly outside in rows 12 inches apart, 12 to 1 inch deep, and 1 inch apart.

How to harvest: See if the radish is ready to be harvested by checking the roots. They should be roughly one inch in length. To remove the radish from the ground, pull straight up.

Recommended varieties: Watermelon, Daikon, French Breakfast

ROSEMARY

Top Companions That Benefit Rosemary

- **Alyssum** attracts many pollinators and beneficial insects.
- **Lavender** has similar care requirements.
- **Strawberries** and **Rosemary** work well together as they improve each other's fertility.

Plants That Are Not Friendly With Rosemary

- **Mint** likes wet and damp soil, while rosemary likes dry and drained soil. They also compete for space.
- Rosemary gets root rot reasonably quickly. Because of that, **Pumpkins** can hinder the health of this herb.

Overview

Plant type: Herb

Soil pH: Slightly Acidic to Neutral

Bloom time: Summer

Maturity time: Six to twelve months

When to plant: Eight to ten weeks before the last spring frost.

How to plant: Plant seedlings or cuttings in well-drained soil.

How to harvest: Snip off stems.

Recommended varieties: Tuscan Blue, Arp

SAGE

Top Companions That Sage Benefits

- Sage helps deter carrot rust flies from **Carrots**.
- Sage deters **Strawberries** pests, and it is said to enhance the flavor.
- Sage deters flea beetles and attracts beneficial insecs for the **Tomatoes**.

Plants That Are Not Friendly With Sage

- **Onions, Garlic,** and **Chives** thrive in a different environment than sage. Therefore, planting them together won't yield a bountiful harvest.
- **Rue** inhibits the growth of sage.
- **Wormwood** is harmful to sage.

Overview

Plant type: Herb

Soil pH: Slightly Acidic to Neutral

Bloom time: Summer

Maturity time: Seventy-five days

When to plant: One to two weeks before the last spring frost.

How to plant: Plant seeds about 1/8 inch deep in damp garden soil or seed-starting mix.

How to harvest: Remove little sprigs or pinch off leaves from the plant.

Recommended varieties: Tricolor

WINTER SQUASH AND PUMPKINS

Top Companions That Benefit Pumpkins and Squash

- **Beans, Corn**, and **Peas** improve soil conditions.
- **Onions, Chives**, and **Garlic** keep pests at bay.
- **Radishes** help loosen the soil.

Plants That Are Not Friendly With Pumpkins and Squash

- **Melons** and **Zucchini** are heavy feeders that remove soil nutrients.
- **Potatoes** and **Carrots** may damage the roots of pumpkins.

Overview

Plant type: Vegetable

Soil pH: Slightly Acidic to Neutral

Bloom time: Summer

Maturity time: Eighty to 110 days

When to plant: Two to four weeks before your last spring frost date.

How to plant: Sow seeds 1 inch deep in flat ground, 2 to 3 feet apart.

How to harvest: Carefully cut the squash off the vine with a sharp knife or scissors; do not damage the stem or the vines.

Recommended varieties: Honeybaby, Butterscotch, Tuffy

SPINACH

Top Companions That Benefit Spinach

- **Beans** fix nitrogen in the soil and provide shade.
- **Radishes** and **Asparagus** help loosen the soil.
- **Strawberries** deter harmful pests and attract beneficial pollinators.

Plants That Are Not Friendly With Spinach

- **Potatoes** take much-needed nutrients away from the spinach.
- **Pumpkins** and **Melons** take away sunlight.
- **Fennel** emits harmful elements. It is best to steer clear of the fennel in your vegetable garden.

Overview

Plant type: Vegetable

Soil pH: Neutral

Bloom time: Spring

Maturity time: Thirty-seven to forty-five days

When to plant: As soon as the ground warms to 40°F.

How to plant: Plant seeds 1/2 inch deep and cover them with 1/2 inch of soil. Plant 12 to 18 inches apart in rows or scatter across a large row or bed.

How to harvest: Remove the flower or seed heads.

Recommended varieties: Baby-leaf, Savoy-leaf, Semi-savoy

STRAWBERRIES

Top Companions That Benefit Strawberries

- **Beans** fix nitrogen in the soil.
- **Beets** and **Radishes** help loosen the soil.
- **Chives, Mint,** and **Borage** deter pests while attracting beneficial insects.
- **Lettuce** and **Spinach** create a good ground cover.

Plants That Are Not Friendly With Strawberries

- **Cabbage** and **Kale** feed on similar nutrients and attract pests.
- **Potatoes, Tomatoes**, and **Peppers** take nutrients from the soil.

Overview

Plant type: Fruit

Soil pH: Slightly Acidic to Neutral

Bloom time: Varies

Maturity time: Four to six weeks after blossoming

When to plant: Spring

How to plant: Plants should be spaced 18 inches apart to allow for runners and 4 feet between rows.

How to harvest: Cut or snap the stem above the fruit when it is ripe.

Recommended varieties: Cardinal, Sable, Tristar

TOMATOES

Top Companions That Benefit Tomatoes

- **Basil** helps repel tomato hornworms.
- **Chervil** keeps the slugs at bay.
- **Garlic** helps repel spider mites and aphids. It is also known to help the flavor of the tomato.
- **Radishes** and **Asparagus** loosen the soil.

Plants That Are Not Friendly With Tomatoes

- **Brussels Sprouts** contain chemicals that inhibit the tomatoes growth.
- **Cabbage** attracts harmful insects.
- **Corn** takes away the much-needed sun from the tomatoes.

Overview

Plant type: Vegetable/Fruit

Soil pH: Acidic, Slightly Acidic to Neutral

Bloom time: Summer

Maturity time: Sixty to 100 days

When to plant: Spring

How to plant: Sow seeds 1/2 inch deep in small trays.

How to harvest: Use shears to cut off the tomato and brush off the soil.

Recommended varieties: Early Girl, Floramerica, Brandywine

ZUCCHINI/SUMMER SQUASH

Top Companions That Benefit Zucchini/Summer Squash

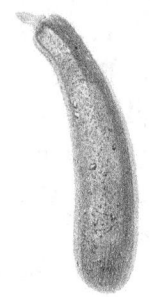

- **Beans** fix nitrogen in the soil.
- **Garlic** and **Borage** deter pests like aphids.
- **Lettuce** and **Spinach** help keep the soil moist by providing excellent ground cover.
- **Radishes** keep squash bugs, cucumber beetles, and aphids at bay.

Plants That Are Not Friendly With Zucchini/Summer Squash

- **Carrots** and **Beets** slow down growth.
- **Potatoes** use up needed nutrients.

Overview

Plant type: Vegetable

Soil pH: Slightly Acidic to Neutral

Bloom time: Summer

Maturity time: Forty-five to fifty-five days

When to plant: Spring

How to plant: Sow seeds 1 inch deep and 2 to 3 inches apart in level ground.

How to harvest: Vegetables should be cut (not broken) from the vine using a sharp knife to avoid injuring the plant's fragile stem. Leave a minimum of one inch of stem attached to the fruit.

Recommended varieties: Cashflow, Goldbar, Sunburst

. . .

Benefits of Using Marigold in Your Companion Garden

I would rank marigolds as the number one flower to plant in your garden. They are not only beautiful flowers, but they also have many benefits.

Marigolds not only attract pollinators but also attract many beneficial insects. Insects such as parasitic wasps, lacewings, and ladybugs. These insects help control the pests that are harmful to your garden. There is some evidence that says marigolds may help in repelling certain pests. These pests include Mexican bean beetles, white flies, and cabbage moths.

Other benefits of marigolds include their ability to create chemicals that are very harmful to nematodes. Nematodes are annoying microscopic worms that damage vegetable roots.

Marigolds are useful more than just in the garden. It is commonly used to make soaps, perfumes, and yellow dye. Once the growing season is over, if you have marigolds left, you can simply cut them down and drop them back into the garden to be decomposed as organic matter.

ITEMS TO CONSIDER

Before you start planning your companion raised bed garden, it is vital to carefully consider the following points:

- Companion plants
- The season of the crop
- The right time to plant
- Light, and soil requirements of the crop

Do not rush into planting because you have a passion for it. Prevention is better than a cure, right? Getting all the necessary information before planting is also better than trying to fix mistakes afterwards. Use the table below to check if you have acquired all the necessary information. Tick each section to verify if you have the corresponding information.

Crop Name:		
Information	**Information Acquired**	**Notes**
Soil Requirement		
Water Requirement		
Sunlight Requirement		
Soil pH		
Raised Bed Size		
Possible Pests		
Possible Disease		
Possible Weeds		

Bloom Time		
Growth Time		
When to Plant		
How to Plant		
How to Harvest		

CONCLUSION

We have now successfully learned which fruit and vegetables grow well together. We also know the bloom time, when to plant, how to plant, and how to harvest them. In the same way that defenders are paired together in defense, some crops are grown together for the benefit of both plants. I think you are ready to start your garden, but it would be remiss of me not to warn you about the common slipups. The next chapter will discuss the common mistakes gardeners make and how to avoid them.

8

COMMON MISTAKES TO AVOID

I have heard many people say that mistakes are inevitable, but some mistakes are avoidable. In this chapter, I will discuss mistakes almost all gardeners make and how to avoid them.

These are a compilation of my own experiences and other common mistakes gardeners make. This book has been structured so you have all the information you need to avoid mistakes. I want you to have a prosperous and flourishing garden all year round. So I am giving you the "A–Z" of gardening.

FIFTEEN COMMON TRAPS TO AVOID

A few typical blunders to avoid when starting out will save you time and work while also increasing your chances of a successful harvest.

1. Planting Too Early

Keep calm before starting your garden. Getting your hands in the dirt and planting seeds months before the last frost date is appealing. Small seeds need more space when growing. They become stressed if forced to remain indoors because they were planted too early. If you plant in beds before time, your seeds may not get the right amount of sunlight and soil nutrients.

2. Picking a Bad Spot

Working in a vegetable garden on a cool spring or fall day is pleasurable. Still, if your garden is not in a convenient spot, you may not want to visit every day. Picking the right location will help your crops get the right amount of water and sun exposure. Plus, you will be able to fence them appropriately against pests.

3. Skimping on Soil

Taking note of the type of soil in your garden is crucial to the health of your plants, which rely on an acid-alkalinity balance. Apart from nitrogen, phosphorus, and potassium, the three primary nutrients that must be present in the soil, other secondary nutrients like micronutrients and good microbes are also beneficial. So, do not overwork your soil or work on it too early, or the earth will lose natural nutrients, and you will have to fight poor soil all season.

4. Not Harvesting

Your garden will slow down if you do not harvest plants when they are ready to be picked. If a plant's branches are already heavy with cucumbers or peppers, they will not produce more. Harvesting some herbs like cilantro and basil at intervals is beneficial, and cutting the plants' tops stimulates them to spread out and become fuller.

5. Planting Too Much

A classic beginner's mistake is planting more than you can eat or care for. It takes time and effort to maintain a vegetable garden. It is more fun to succeed with a small garden than battle with a large one. You can become overwhelmed by too much variety.

6. Ignoring Spacing

Some vegetables that are large or bushy, such as corn and beans, will require more space when they reach maturity. If you pack these vegetables in too tightly, they will not get enough light or air, which will lead to disease and smaller harvests. Some of the plants that require a lot of space include squash and cucumber, and I wouldn't recommend planting these if you have a small area to work with.

7. Not Staggering Harvest Times

The most effective method for ensuring a continual harvest may be succession planting. For example, instead of planting one large row at the start of the season, you can lengthen your yield by planting short rows every two weeks. Keep in mind that planting maize and beans in long rows will give a better harvest.

8. Putting Off Maintenance

Weeding, feeding, and particularly watering must be done regularly. Most of us shower, drink water, and clean up after a day's work. That's body maintenance. So, ensure you weed and water your garden regularly. Do not forget to weed appropriately and water properly.

9. Not Fencing

If you do not want your garden to be cleared overnight by a rabbit or some other pest, protect it by fencing in your crops. The importance of a well-built fence cannot be overemphasized. Your animal concerns determine the type of barricade you need. You may need a high barrier or electric fence for jumping rodents like deer or a buried fence for rodents that dig in the ground like rabbits.

10. Ignoring Little Problems

My mom would say that not every problem in the garden requires all your energy, but do not ignore small issues either. A minor problem may not cause any problems today but may lead to something worse if not taken care of. So, treat the minor problems soon. It is better to be safe than sorry.

11. Planting Without Planning

Ensure you have a plan. If all the boxes provided in the table in Chapter 7 are not checked, it may not be the right time to start a garden. Get all the necessary information first.

12. Over-Fertilization

I know that eating is good, but did you know that overeating is harmful? Your system will become destabilized, and you may even fall sick. Over-fertilizing your soil will not make a difference; the correct quantity is enough.

13. Use of Synthetic Fertilizers

Synthetic fertilizers are cheap, yes! Run from them as far as you can, though. They are potentially dangerous. Determine whether or not the fertilizer you want to buy is organic.

14. Too Much Water

Just as over-fertilization is bad, over-watering is bad too. You would not force yourself to drink five liters of water when you can only finish one. So, please do not give your soil more water than it can cope with.

15. Forgetting the Sun

Sunlight is something that many homeowners overlook. Plants, like us, require sunshine. However, keep in mind that certain plants prefer shade.

TAKEAWAY

Most of the mistakes mentioned here are easy to make and easy to avoid. The only difference between a gardener that will make these mistakes and a gardener that will prevent them is that they pay attention. As long as you pay attention to details, you are on your way to becoming an excellent gardener.

CONCLUSION

Getting to this point from the beginning of this book has been an exciting journey I would love to do again. Companion planting will not only act as a companion to you in your garden but as a light to help you have a successful harvest.

Before reading this book, you may have had little or no knowledge of soil composition, water and sunlight requirements, and how to prepare beds. But now, you have a knowledge of these things and know how to manage pests, diseases, and weeds. Of course, the best part is knowing what crops to pair and the common mistakes to avoid. So, you can call yourself a gardener.

I am still enjoying my garden, even when I realized my space would not contain every crop I wanted to plant. There's no bigger joy than knowing that I eat fresh and chemical-free food. Apart from the food benefits of my garden, I visit my garden regularly to get fresh air. I get inspired inside my garden, and I know it will work for others.

So, I have a little task for you. I want you to document your plans and progress. Get yourself a diary and document your journey from the first planting until harvesting day. If you can record yourself, please do. Edit your videos, add comments, and make it look like a documentary. Well, it is a documentary, hypothetically speaking. I would love to see and hear about your progress.

Join our Facebook page *The Gardening Support Community* to interact with fellow gardeners, ask questions, and support one another.

Please drop a review if this book has inspired you, shaped you, and improved you. I will be happy to hear from you. See you again some other time.

To leave a review go to https://www.amazon.com/review/review-your-purchases or scan the QR code.

JUST FOR YOU

A FREE GIFT TO OUR READERS

Scan the QR code below to get The Ultimate Gardening Tool Kit.

REFERENCES

10 Biggest Vegetable Gardening Mistakes We've All Made. (2022, February 9). The Spruce. https://www.thespruce.com/biggest-vegetable-gardening-mistakes-1402993

10 golden rules for watering. (2008). Gardena. https://www.gardena.com/int/garden-life/garden-magazine/10-golden-rules-for-watering/

13 Common Garden Weeds. (2022). Almanac.Com. https://www.almanac.com/content/common-garden-weeds

A. (2020, April 4). 5 Common Gardening Mistakes Homeowners should Avoid. Balcony Garden Web. https://balconygardenweb.com/5-gardening-mistakes-homeowner-avoid/

A. (2021, August 5). 29 Best Potato Companion Plants (& The Worst). GP. Retrieved May 3, 2022, from https://growers-planet.com/potato-companion-plants/

Basil. (2021). Almanac.Com. https://www.almanac.com/plant/basil

BBC Gardeners' World Magazine. (2021, February 16). How to grow borage. https://www.gardenersworld.com/how-to/grow-plants/how-to-grow-borage/

Beck, A. (2020, July 23). Do You Really Need to Fertilize Your Plants? Here's What You Need to Know. Better Homes & Gardens. https://www.bhg.com/gardening/yard/garden-care/why-you-should-fertilize-plants/

Bell Peppers. (2021). Almanac.Com. https://www.almanac.com/plant/bell-peppers

Boeckmann, C. (2015a). Brussels Sprouts. Almanac.Com. https://www.almanac.com/plant/brussels-sprouts

Boeckmann, C. (2015b). Cabbage. Almanac.Com. https://www.almanac.com/plant/cabbage

Boeckmann, C. (2015c). Corn. Almanac.Com. https://www.almanac.com/plant/corn

Boeckmann, C. (2015d). Eggplants. Almanac.Com. https://www.almanac.com/plant/eggplants

Boeckmann, C. (2015e). Kale. Almanac.Com. https://www.almanac.com/plant/kale

Boeckmann, C. (2015f). Strawberries. Almanac.Com. https://www.almanac.com/plant/strawberries

Boeckmann, C. (2015g). Broccoli. Almanac.Com. https://www.almanac.com/plant/broccoli

Boeckmann, C. (2015h). Asparagus. Almanac.Com. https://www.almanac.com/plant/asparagus

Boeckmann, C. (2015I). Beets. Almanac.Com. https://www.almanac.com/plant/beets

Bradbury, K. (2010, September 5). Understanding Soil Types for Vegetable Gardens. GrowVeg. https://www.growveg.com/guides/understanding-soil-types-for-vegetable-gardens/#:%7E:text=Soil%20is%20made%20from%20three,are%20suited%20to%20different%20soils.

Class, M. (2020, November 8). Carrot Companion Planting Guide: 7 Plants to Pair With Carrots. MasterClass. https://www.masterclass.com/articles/carrot-companion-planting-guide#quiz-0

Claydon, S. (2021, March 10). *Health Effects of Pesticides. Pesticide Action Network UK.* https://www.pan-uk.org/health-effects-of-pesticides/

Companion Planting Guide for Vegetables. (2021). Almanac.Com. https://www.almanac.com/companion-planting-guide-vegetables

Cowles, D. (2021, December 26). *Top 10 Reasons to Grow Your Own Organic Food. Unsustainable.* https://www.unsustainablemagazine.com/top-10-reasons-to-grow-your-own-organic-food/

Dore, J. (2010). *Trap Cropping to Control Pests. GrowVeg.* https://www.growveg.co.uk/guides/trap-cropping-to-control-pests/

E. (2022, April 30). *Companion Planting Square Foot Gardening [Complete Guide] - Gardening Tips And Tricks. Gardening Tips and Tricks.* https://gardeningelsa.com/companion-planting-square-foot-gardening

Editors, T. (2015a). *Cantaloupes. Almanac.Com.* https://www.almanac.com/plant/cantaloupes

Editors, T. (2015b). *Carrots. Almanac.Com.* https://www.almanac.com/plant/carrots

Editors, T. (2015c). *Chives. Almanac.Com.* https://www.almanac.com/plant/chives

Editors, T. (2015d). *Cilantro (Coriander). Almanac.Com.* https://www.almanac.com/plant/cilantro-coriander

Editors, T. (2015e). *Cucumbers. Almanac.Com.* https://www.almanac.com/plant/cucumbers

Editors, T. (2015f). *Dill. Almanac.Com.* https://www.almanac.com/plant/dill

Editors, T. (2015g). *Garlic. Almanac.Com.* https://www.almanac.com/plant/garlic

Editors, T. (2015h). *Green Beans. Almanac.Com.* https://www.almanac.com/plant/beans

Editors, T. (2015i). *Lettuce. Almanac.Com.* https://www.almanac.com/plant/lettuce

Editors, T. (2015j). Mint. Almanac.Com. https://www.almanac.com/plant/mint

Editors, T. (2015k). Onions. Almanac.Com. https://www.almanac.com/plant/onions

Editors, T. (2015l). Peas. Almanac.Com. https://www.almanac.com/plant/peas

Editors, T. (2015m). Potatoes. Almanac.Com. https://www.almanac.com/plant/potatoes

Editors, T. (2015n). Pumpkins. Almanac.Com. https://www.almanac.com/plant/pumpkins

Editors, T. (2015o). Radishes. Almanac.Com. https://www.almanac.com/plant/radishes

Editors, T. (2015p). Rosemary. Almanac.Com. https://www.almanac.com/plant/rosemary

Editors, T. (2015q). Sage. Almanac.Com. https://www.almanac.com/plant/sage

Editors, T. (2015r). Spinach. Almanac.Com. https://www.almanac.com/plant/spinach

Editors, T. (2015s). Tomatoes. Almanac.Com. https://www.almanac.com/plant/tomatoes

Editors, T. (2015t). Winter Squash. Almanac.Com. https://www.almanac.com/plant/winter-squash

Editors, T. (2015u). Zucchini. Almanac.Com. https://www.almanac.com/plant/zucchini

Eyres, H. (2019, August 23). Polyculture Gardening: A Healthy, Brilliant Way to Grow Food. Garden and Happy. https://gardenandhappy.com/polyculture/

Gardening, C. A. (2021, May 15). Most Common Vegetable Garden Diseases and Solutions. Clean Air Gardening. https://www.cleanairgardening.com/most-common-vegetable-garden-diseases-and-solutions/

Guide to Garden Watering Methods. (2022, June 9). MiracleGro. https://www.miraclegro.com/en-us/library/water-wise-gardening/guide-garden-watering-methods

Hassani, N. (2021, November 29). The Basics of Companion Planting Garden Crops. The Spruce. https://www.thespruce.com/companion-planting-with-chart-5025124

Hayes, K. (2021, September 17). 12 Common Garden Pests in the United States and How to Control Them. FineGardening. https://www.finegardening.com/collection/how-to-control-12-garden-pests-in-the-united-states

Heber, G. (2022, January 1). How to Grow Leeks. Gardener's Path. https://gardenerspath.com/plants/vegetables/grow-leeks/

Hessong, A. (2020, November 17). What Does Tilling Soil Mean? Home Guides | SF Gate. https://homeguides.sfgate.com/tilling-soil-mean-43382.html

Holmes, K. (2022, May 30). The Garden Decoder: What Is a 'Potager'? Gardenista. https://www.gardenista.com/posts/garden-decoder-what-is-companion-planting-gardening-best-vegetable-companions/

How to Build a Raised Bed. (2019, July 1). Garden Topsoil Direct. https://www.gardentopsoildirect.co.uk/gardening-tips/building-a-raised-bed

Jones, S. (2018, September 28). The History Of Companion Planting. Growing Guides. https://growing-guides.co.uk/the-history-of-companion-planting/

JOWAHEER, R. (2021, March 12). 10 steps for making your own compost heap at home. Country Living. https://www.countryliving.com/uk/homes-interiors/gardens/a23333516/how-to-make-compost-heap-home/

Kanuckel, A. (2022, June 6). 8 Best Homemade Natural Garden Fertilizers. Farmers' Almanac. https://www.farmersalmanac.com/8-homemade-garden-fertilizers-24258

Lofgren, K. (2021, December 29). How to Grow Chervil. Gardener's Path. https://gardenerspath.com/plants/herbs/grow-chervil/

Love The Garden. (2022). Why use organic and natural pesticides? https://www.lovethegarden.com/uk-en/article/why-use-organic-and-natural-pesticides

Mama, P. (2018, July 11). Companion Planting Basics. PreparednessMama. https://preparednessmama.com/companion-planting-basics

Markham, D. (2021, April 6). 8 Natural & Homemade Insecticides: Save Your Garden Without Killing the Earth. Treehugger. https://www.treehugger.com/natural-homemade-insecticides-save-your-garden-without-killing-earth-4858819

Neveln, V. (2022, January 19). How to Test Your Garden Soil's pH Level in 4 Simple Steps. Better Homes & Gardens. https://www.bhg.com/gardening/yard/soil/how-to-test-your-soil/

Nick, J., & Nick, J. (2021, November 2). The Pros and Cons of Square Foot Gardening. Good Housekeeping. https://www.goodhousekeeping.com/home/gardening/a20706747/square-foot-gardening/

nmhealthysoil. (2020). The many benefits of healthy soil. https://www.nmhealthysoil.org/benefits/

Nolan, A. (2020, September 3). What Is the Purpose of Compost? Garden Guides. https://www.gardenguides.com/12312429-what-is-the-purpose-of-compost.html

Pierre-Louis, K. (2018, September 5). The Bugs Are Coming, and They'll Want More of Our Food. The New York Times. https://www.nytimes.com/2018/08/30/climate/insects-eating-more-crops.html

Planet Natural. (2018a, May 4). Gardening Terms (Glossary). https://www.planetnatural.com/vegetable-gardening-guru/garden-terms/

Planet Natural. (2018b, November 19). How to Improve Garden Soil Quality. https://www.planetnatural.com/organic-gardening-guru/soil/

Rhoades, H. (2021). StackPath. GardeningKnowHow. https://www.gardeningknowhow.com/edible/herbs/mustard/growing-mustard-seed.htm

Smith And Weeks. (2017, January 27). Disease Management in the Home Vegetable Garden. Center for Agriculture, Food, and the Environment. https://ag.umass.edu/home-lawn-garden/fact-sheets/disease-management-in-home-vegetable-garden

Staff, G. M. (2012, May 8). New study reveals home gardening statistics. Greenhouse Management. https://www.greenhousemag.com/article/greenhouse-management-new-study-home-gardening-statistics/

Stanborough, R. M. J. (2020, June 17). Seed, Soil, and Sun: Discovering the Many Healthful Benefits of Gardening. Healthline. https://www.healthline.com/health/healthful-benefits-of-gardening

Styles, R. (2014, April 17). Secrets of Prince Charles' gorgeous Highgrove garden revealed in new book. Mail Online. https://www.dailymail.co.uk/femail/article-2605972/Secrets-Prince-Charles-gorgeous-Highgrove-garden-revealed-new-book.html

Taylor, C. (2019, December 19). 7 Homemade Fungicides That Will Save Your Garden Plants. MorningChores. https://morningchores.com/homemade-fungicides/

Teagasc. (2020). Teagasc | Agriculture and Food Development Authority. Horticultural Weeds. https://www.teagasc.ie/media/website/crops/horticulture/vegetables/Illustrated_Guide_to_Horticultural_Weeds_2020.pdf

Tilley, N. (2021a). Watering The Garden – Tips On How And When To Water The Garden. GardeningKnowHow. https://www.gardeningknowhow.com/garden-how-to/watering/watering-garden.htm

Tilley, N. (2021b). What Is A Weed: Weed Info And Control Methods In Gardens. GardeningKnowHow. https://www.gardeningknowhow.com/plant-problems/weeds/what-is-a-weed.htm

Universal, G. (2018, February 21). Sunlight Guide for Home Grown Produce. Garden Universal. https://www.gardenuniversal.co.uk/growing-tips/sunlight-guide/

van Uitert, M. (2015, April 2). How to Grow Food in Small Spaces: 8 Tips That Work (Even if Your Space is. Nourishing Joy. https://nourishingjoy.com/how-to-grow-food-in-small-spaces/

Waddington, E. (2022, March 14). 15 Reasons To Grow Marigolds In The Vegetable Garden. Rural Sprout. https://www.ruralsprout.com/marigolds-in-the-vegetable-garden/

Walliser, J. (2022, May 6). Guide to vegetable garden pests: Identification and organic controls. Savvy Gardening. https://savvygardening.com/guide-to-vegetable-garden-pests/

Walls-Thumma, D. (2020, November 17). What Is the Purpose of a Compost Heap? Home Guides | SF Gate. https://homeguides.sfgate.com/purpose-compost-heap-78411.html

White, A. (2022, February 26). Your Ultimate Guide to Square Foot Gardening. Gardener's Path. https://gardenerspath.com/how-to/design/guide-to-square-foot-gardening/

www.ingramcontent.com/pod-product-compliance
Lightning Source LLC
Chambersburg PA
CBHW070705130626
46553CB00005B/1842